Also by Gary Ferraro

The Two Worlds of Kamau (1978)

The Cultural Dimension of International Business (1990, 1994, 1998, 2002)

Cultural Anthropology: An Applied Perspective (1992, 1995, 1998, 2001)

Anthropology: An Applied Perspective (1994)

Applying Cultural Anthropology: Readings (1998)

Global Brains

Knowledge and Competencies
for the 21st Century

Gary Ferraro

Intercultural Associates, Inc
Charlotte, North Carolina

Editor: Lorne Lassiter
Copy Editor   Chris Harrington
Formatter: Celia Hamilton
Cover Design: Christy Burch

3 2280 00755 8570

Publisher's Cataloging-in-Publication
(Provided by Quality Books, Inc.)

Ferraro, Gary P.
   Global brains: knowledge and competencies
for the 21st century / by Gary Ferraro. -- 1st ed.
p. cm.
   Includes bibliographical references and index.
   ISBN 0-9712388-0-4
   1. International business enterprises--Social
aspects. 2. Intercultural communication. 3.
Corporate culture--Cross-cultural studies.
4. Success in business. I. Title

HD2755.5.F47 2001   302.3'5
                           QBI01-200800

For Hanes, Kathryn, Lydia, Matt, Preston, and Stefan, and, of course, Avery and Mitch, the next generation.

Contents

Preface

It is embarrassing to have to state the obvious, but our world of the 21st century is experiencing extraordinarily rapid culture change. While commentators have, no doubt, made similar statements during most periods of human history, the nature of the change that is engulfing today's world is quantitatively and qualitatively different from the past. In the last decade there has been a worldwide opening up of markets, lowering of tariff barriers, and privatization of enterprises in many countries throughout the world. And, at the same time, the world is up to its eyeballs in a flurry of new information technology, which is allowing communication to occur at hyper speeds. Mobile phones, pagers, voice mail, and Global Positioning Satellites are just some of the gizmos responsible for the meltdown of traditional boundaries. Keep in mind that less than a decade ago, a mere handful of people in the world were using email!

Some have suggested that in the face of this revolution of free-flowing goods and ideas, it won't be long before all of the world's cultures will be homogenized down into a single culture. They have argued that this rapid flow of money, commodities, and information to every corner of the world, if allowed to continue unchecked, will eventually eradicate cultural differences. However, don't hold your breath waiting for that to happen anytime soon. One only needs to look at all of the tensions, conflicts, and hotspots in the world to realize that people are not willing to give up their cultural distinctiveness. Traditional cultures are not only surviving the information revolution, they are making some creative adaptations to it. To illustrate, the Middle Eastern airline, Gulf Air, uses a Global Positioning Satellite (GPS) to inform its Islamic passengers exactly where the holy city of Mecca is located in relation to the airplane, so they will know in which direction to face when praying in the aisle of the airplane.

Thus, owing to the increased opportunities for exchanging goods, services, and ideas, the world is a very different place than it was in the mid-1980s. And yet the magnitude of cultural diversity throughout the world has in no way diminished. If any thing, we have seen many cultural groups become even more defensive, nationalistic, and strident. Western business people can no longer expect to be competitive in world markets, as they were in the past, by insisting that potential customers come to them. If the United States is to survive as an economic leader, Americans will need to immerse themselves in the complex, rapidly moving, and very diverse global marketplace. They will require a solid knowledge of cultural differences, familiarity with the many variations in business practices, second language competence, and a host of cognitive skills essential for adjusting to different parts of the world. The successful leader in the world economy today has to be better prepared and more competent than ever before. But it is more than that. Today's global leaders need to be capable in ways quite different from their predecessors. They need to have a *global mindset*, which involves seeing and understanding the world differently than they were conditioned to seeing it. They need to be able to develop and interpret decisions and strategies that are not dependent on the assumptions of a single country or culture. And, they need to be able to implement those decisions and strategies effectively in different cultures throughout the world. In short, they need to develop global brains. How well equipped are you for competing in this rapidly changing global economy of the 21st century?

This book is designed for those interested in becoming important players in the world economy in the new millenium. As the subtitle implies, the book focuses on two broad areas. First, we will look at the knowledge base (concepts, generalizations, and insights) the globally savvy leaders will need to understand and apply to business problems in the years to come. And second, the book explores in considerable depth those skills and competencies essential for navigating successfully through the turbulent waters of the new global economy.

Americans, who deal with time very precisely, tend to be impatient because, after all, time is money. We are accustomed to punctuality, meeting deadlines, and quick results. When we purchase a manual on how to install and operate a new word processing program for our personal computer, we expect that we will be totally "up and running" in a matter of hours. The development of a global mindset, however, is a different kind of animal. The insights, concepts, and competencies discussed in Global Brains will not be fully operational in a matter of hours or even days after finishing the book. The insights contained herein need to be understood, digested, and applied in a number of different cultural contexts over the long run. They are, in other words, a set of understandings and skills that should guide you throughout your professional life and career.

Global Brains takes a conceptual approach to understanding the cultural dimension of the global economy. That is, it provides you with a set of concepts derived from the comparative study of culture and enables you to see how they can be applied to the world of international business. But, this is not a cookbook, whereby, if you follow a series of 19 easy-to-follow steps, you will be able to avoid any cross-cultural problem when operating in the global economy. Instead, the book is predicated on the fact that it is impossible for anyone to ever master *all* of the cultural knowledge needed to solve *every* potential cross-cultural problem that might come your way. We encourage you to understand the various *concepts* as fully as possible so you will be able to apply them to real-life situations in the future. In order to help you with these applications, the book draws heavily on the use of cross-cultural scenarios. These are realistic mini-encounters between people from different cultures who fail to communicate because of their different value assumptions. These scenarios are used to introduce each of the ten value dimensions in chapters three and four. In addition, chapters two through seven end with three scenarios in the form of a cross-cultural quiz. You are encouraged to read and analyze these scenarios so as to give you practice at analyzing potential cross-cultural misunderstandings. The better you get at analyzing these hypothetical, but realistic, scenarios, the better you will become at diagnosing real-life cross-cultural miscommunications in the future. The correct answers to each of the scenarios at the end of chapters two through seven are found in the appendix.

Finally, this book reflects the ideas and insights gained from a 30-year career as a cross-cultural researcher, teacher, and consultant. There have been many people along the way (too numerous to single out) who have helped shape the ideas in this book. These include my many mentors in graduate school and beyond, my colleagues at the University of North Carolina at Charlotte, the many cultural anthropologists and business professionals who have commented on my past writings, and the thousands of students and trainees who have provided valuable feedback over the years. To all of these many people I give my heartfelt thanks, along with the acknowledgement that I would never have been able to write Global Brains without their insights, guidance, and encouragement.

Gary Ferraro
Charlotte, NC

CHAPTER 1

WHY GLOBAL BRAINS?

The world---and the world of business---has changed dramatically in the last 15 years. While the old adage that "there is nothing as constant as change" was as true in our distant past as it is today, the nature of the changes that have occurred since the mid-1980s have been profound and far reaching. The end of the cold war, coupled with the rapid onset of the information age, have unleashed forces that are transforming not only the way we do business in the world today, but indeed the very nature of both corporations and the countries in which they are operating. These vast changes are often subsumed under the general heading of "globalization," a term often used, frequently misunderstood, and capable of generating heated political discussions.

According to <u>New York Times</u> correspondent Thomas Friedman (1999), globalization is not just a passing trend, but rather is a worldwide phenomenon that involves a new type of integration of markets, technology, and information that is oblivious to both national and cultural borders. Globalization, driven by free-market capitalism, involves lowering tariff barriers, privatizing enterprises, and deregulating national economies. The result of the globalization of markets is that goods and services from all over the world are making their way into other cultures; powerful trading alliances, such as NAFTA and the European Economic Union, are emerging; customers from all parts of the world are demanding quality goods, regardless of their country of origin; time needed to develop and deliver new products has been shrinking; and there has been a significant increase in the number of mergers and strategic alliances between former competitors in order to gain access to new markets, new technologies, and skilled workers.

At the same time that world trade barriers are falling, there is a concurrent revolution going on in the world of information technology. In the mid-1980s only a handful of people in the world could operate a computer. Today, computers are nearly as common in the home as televisions were in the 1970s. Moreover, the development of digitization, fiber optics, satellite communication, and the Internet now enables people to communicate with one another instantaneously.

We can cite a number of "leading indicators" that globalization is not a figment of our imagination:

- Direct U.S. investment abroad totals approximately $1 trillion, while foreign investment in the United States is $3 trillion.
- Over half of the doctoral degrees in engineering and mathematics granted by U.S. universities are awarded to non-U.S. citizens.
- Foreign-owned firms in the United States employ roughly 5 million people, while U.S. firms abroad employ about 100 million workers.
- There is more Coca-Cola sold in Japan than in the United States.
- BMWs are being made in South Carolina, and Nike running shoes are being made in Taiwan.

- McDonalds operates over 12,000 burger restaurants in more than 70 different countries.

It has become a cliché to say that the world is becoming a "global village." Rapid technological developments in transportation and communications in recent decades have brought the peoples of the world closer together in ways that we could barely imagine just a decade ago. The globalization of many companies has made it difficult to determine the "home country" of certain brands. Unfortunately, despite the growing world interdependency, there has not been a parallel revolution in cross-cultural understanding among all the peoples of the world. And, of course, no one could argue that we have witnessed any degree of cultural homogenization of world populations. Instead, this rapid globalization of world economies is making the need for understanding the cultural dimension of our business enterprises increasingly *more* imperative, not less. Nor does working, as many of us do today, with ultra high-speed technology in the world of e-commerce absolve us from having to understand the cultures (values and behaviors) of our customers, clients, suppliers, overseas work forces, or business partners. The cultural differences found in today's world are every bit as important in our cyber-businesses as they were when we were communicating on stationery with a quill-tip pen.

For the last several hundred years, companies lived or died by the availability of natural resources, such as steel or plastics, which were used to manufacture their products. With rapid globalization, however, a major shift has taken place away from physical commodities toward information. In today's world, it is people, and the knowledge they possess, that constitute the real competitive advantage. Multinational corporations are, at long last, beginning to realize that their corporate health directly depends upon their success in the global arena. As a result, international experience and successful overseas assignments are becoming closely associated with upward mobility in the corporation. The people that will not only survive, but thrive, in the 21st century are those willing and able to change their perspectives, develop new competencies, and treat learning as a life-long activity. In short, they need to become what Rosen (2000) refers to as "globally literate."

Given this rapid and dramatic globalization---whether we like it or not---there will be increased opportunities for you (and increased expectations placed on you by your employer) to function in culturally different settings. Global corporations meet their international staffing needs in a number of different ways. In many cases, multinational corporations prefer to use local nationals, if possible, when staffing their overseas operations. The use of local nationals has gained popularity in recent years because they are less expensive than using expatriates, they are popular with host country governments, and they share a common set of cultural and linguistic traits with local employees and customers. Nevertheless, global corporations are reluctant to cut back on using expatriates from home to staff their overseas operations. Expatriates still need to be used for at least two compelling reasons. First, the company is likely to become excessively isolated from its foreign subsidiaries unless it has people from the home office transmitting its corporate culture and concerns. And second, staffing overseas positions with expatriates (rather than local nationals or third-country nationals) provides promising corporate leaders with valuable skills that can best be developed through international experience. That is, if people live and work outside of their own familiar cultural environment, they are more likely to learn a host of strategies and business practices that can be applied at home.

Thus, whether global corporations (your own included) meet their overseas staffing needs through expatriates, local nationals, or third-country nationals, they are constantly looking for the best people to fill those positions. More and more companies are realizing that their future leadership will come from the ranks of those with international/cross-cultural experience. It is not a coincidence that returning Peace Corps volunteers are highly recruited for leadership positions in the private sector. Do you have aspirations for getting to the top of your company or profession? If so, then you must be purposeful in (a) equipping yourself for successful overseas assignments and (b) transferring the competencies learned from those international experiences to higher level assignments within the corporation in the future.

ENHANCING YOUR SKILLS AS A GLOBAL PLAYER

For much of the 20th century, people spent most, if not all, of their careers working for a single employer. In exchange for reasonably hard work and loyalty to the company, the employee was granted a certain measure of job security and the possibility of a pension.

Today, however, the job market has changed dramatically. Workers are laid off, downsized, or rightsized in the company's pursuit of becoming more competitive. Workers, for their part, particularly in a booming economy, show a similar lack of loyalty to their employers, willing to change jobs at the drop of a hat if the right offer comes along. Even in economies such as Japan, Germany, and France, which have had a long history of loyalty between employees and employers, the notion of lifetime employment is quickly becoming a thing of the past.

Today, it is estimated that, on average, people in the United States change employers every five years. They don't see themselves as "jumping ship" as much as "making smart career moves." In such a highly mobile labor market, people are no longer willing to leave themselves to the mercy of their employers. Instead, they are becoming "free agents" (just as with sports figures), capable of *managing themselves as a business* rather than simply selling their labor.

Clearly everyone cannot become a free agent, controlling his or her marketability. The real challenge is to develop marketable *skills* and keep abreast as to how much the market wants those skills. Part of being a desirable "free agent," then, is to manage and market those skills now and into the future.

Just as the labor market is undergoing vast changes, the knowledge base and the skill sets that people will need for successful leadership in the 21st century are changing at an equally dizzying speed. The new breed of leader for the new millenium is a different animal from the traditional leaders of the 20th century. Whereas the traditional manager had a rather narrow perspective, trained in a specialized functional area, the new leaders must have a broad perspective, which is both cross-functional and cross-cultural. Rosabeth Moss Kanter (1995), in her well-received book entitled World Class, suggests that global leaders of the new millenium need to have three preeminent assets: (a) the latest knowledge, (b) the ability to operate at the highest of standards anywhere in the world, and (c) relationships with people all over the world, which provide access to the world's resources. If you are to be successful in the global economy, you must equip yourself with both new *skills* and new *knowledge*. In short, you must develop what, for lack of a better term, we call "global brains."

What does it mean to have global brains? First, being globally savvy involves an ability to communicate effectively with people from a number of different cultural backgrounds, including supervising a culturally diverse workforce, responding appropriately to global customers, and working with suppliers from all over the world. This entails both the ability and the willingness to speak a second language without worrying about making mistakes and generally becoming comfortable when interacting with culturally different people.

Second, the global mindset involves developing a type of "systems thinking," whereby you see the total (integrated) picture of your organization and operations across functional areas and cultural borders.

Third, the global thinker needs to develop certain perceptual skills that will facilitate learning about different cultures. These include, but are not limited to, being open minded, flexible, and patient; tolerating ambiguity; learning from new situations; and adopting good, relevant ideas from wherever they might come.

Fourth, having global brains involves developing those skills and attributes that enhance one's emotional and mental well-being, such as meditation, regular exercise regimens, and other ways of reducing stress levels.

And finally, global brains involves a broad knowledge base, including knowledge of one's own culture, other cultures, corporate cultures, as well as the global economic and geopolitical forces affecting the conduct of business.

None of this will be easy. Bringing about changes in what we know and how we think is never easy. Our tendency is to go with the familiar, the traditional, ways of thinking and behaving. To re-orient ourselves, particularly as adults, will take time, effort, and courage. And, this involves mastering both (a) new knowledge about language, culture, and globalization as well as (b) new skills, competencies, and ways of thinking. But, do we really have a choice? The world is becoming so interconnected (and moving at such a blistering pace) that we either learn to adapt to these new realities or we will be left behind. The good news, however, is that no one expects you to develop a complete set of global brains by a week from Tuesday.

This book is designed to help you acquire both the necessary knowledge and skills needed to become a global player in the 21st century. Reading this book will not, in and of itself, lead to instant success in every aspect of global business. It will, however, provide a solid foundation for starting your journey on mastering the cultural dimension of the global economy. Reading this book, then, is the beginning of a journey that should continue throughout one's entire lifetime.

Our quest for global brains in this book will focus on the two broad areas of *knowledge* and *competencies*. The first part of the book will deal with a cognitive understanding of those concepts and insights you will need to become a world-class player in today's global economy. In the next chapter, we will look at the concept of culture and how it impacts global business. Then in Chapters 3 and 4, we will look at the nature of cultural values, how they play themselves out in different cultures, and their implications for doing business globally. Chapter 5 will examine the question, "Why is language and linguistic competence so essential for acquiring a global mindset?" Chapter 6, which discusses nonverbal communication in a cross-cultural setting, demonstrates why linguistic competence may be necessary, but not sufficient, for becoming globally literate. And finally, we will explore those skills and competencies you will need in order to maximize your chances for success as a player in the global economy. So, if you are ready, let's begin.

CHAPTER 2

CULTURE:
A NEGLECTED DIMENSION

U ntil recently, the conventional view of culture among U.S. corporations was that it was a frill or an afterthought. While it might be nice to know something about different cultures, they argued, it really doesn't have much to do with the successful conduct of global business. Thus, for much of the 20th century western-based corporations concentrated on the economic, political, and legal issues involved in international business while giving short shrift to the cultural dimension. But, as we have come to realize, cultural forces lay at the heart of business relationships and to ignore them can be disastrous.

We can illustrate the impact of cultural differences by briefly exploring one functional area of business, human resources training programs as conducted in the United States and East Asia. After looking at certain fundamental cultural differences between Americans and Asians, we will examine the implications of these cultural differences on conducting training programs in these two parts of the world.

In terms of family structure, American nuclear families encourage children to be responsible for their own major life choices, such as education, career, and marital partner. By way of contrast, the Asian extended families, which play down individual choice, emphasize group harmony and encourage parents and grandparents to take a much more active role in the life decisions of their children. The dominant religion in the United States, Christianity, tends to emphasize individualism, the work ethic, and personal salvation, while Buddhism, Hinduism, and Confucianism stress humility, duty to parents and elders, and harmony with nature and one's fellow humans. In terms of education, Americans tend to emphasize universal educational opportunities, practical learning, and highly competitive classrooms in which the teacher's position, under certain circumstances, can be questioned. In Asia, on the other hand, the teacher's authority and opinions are considered to be above question, and students learn largely through rote memorization.

These cultural differences in terms of family, religion, and education have far-reaching implications when Americans are designing and delivering training programs for Asian employees. To illustrate, since teachers have such high status and unquestioned authority in Asia, trainers should be highly professional and avoid being overly informal. Owing to the cultural emphasis on group harmony, training sessions in Asia should avoid confrontational teaching strategies, which would cause trainees to "lose face." Since the teacher/trainer is considered to have a monopoly on knowledge and wisdom, there is no need to have the trainees set their own objectives for the training session. The very formal and rigid educational systems found in Asia lend themselves to lectures and note-taking, as compared to more participatory strategies used in the United States, such as role playing, small group discussions, and debates. And, it would not be appropriate in Asia to mix trainees according to gender, rank, or age because it would subvert the power structure within the workplace. These are just a few of the ways that major cultural differences between Asians and Americans can impact the design and delivery of training programs across cultures.

WHAT DO WE MEAN BY "CULTURE?"

A large part of developing "global brains" is to become cross-culturally literate. But what do we mean by "culture?" We speak of understanding one's company's "corporate culture," a national culture, a regional cultural, and even "sub-cultures," which are subsets of larger cultures. Although we think we know what we mean by the term "culture," it turns out that it is far more complex and multi-faceted than we at first realize. Biologists use the word culture to refer to microorganisms growing in the bottom of a petri dish, but that is a highly specialized use of the word that has little or no meaning here. In everyday usage, the term culture often refers to the "finer things in life," such as opera, the fine arts, and haute cuisine. We sometimes speak of "highly cultured people" (those who attend symphony concerts, gallery openings, and drink Dom Perignon) and others as "uncultured" (those who watch wrestling on TV and drink cheap beer). But anthropologists (and other social scientists as well) define the term much more broadly to include the total lifeways of a group of people. Thus, when viewed from this more inclusive perspective, "culture" involves much more than playing Brahms on your Steinway or reading a Robert Browning poem. "Culture" includes a group's mundane activities as well, such as brushing one's teeth, shaking hands, driving a car, or eating a hot dog.

While many cross-cultural experts have their own uniquely worded definitions of the term "culture," most of them, when reduced to their basic elements, are saying essentially the same thing. As mentioned in a previous work (Ferraro:2001), I have defined culture as "Everything that people have, think, and do as members of a society." I find this definition helpful, not because it is totally unique, but because the three verbs highlight quite clearly the three major components of any culture. When we speak of "everything that people have," we are referring to their material possessions; "everything that people <u>think</u>" refers to ideas, values, beliefs, and attitudes; while "everything that people <u>do</u>" involves their behavior patterns. Thus, whenever we use the term culture throughout this book, it would be helpful to keep these three basic components in mind.

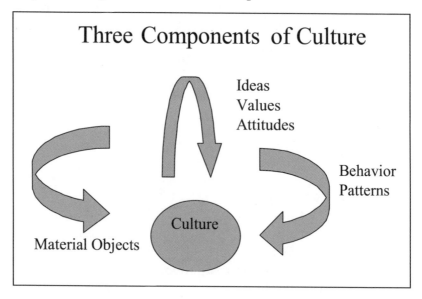

Three Components of Culture

Ideas
Values
Attitudes

Behavior
Patterns

Culture

Material Objects

<u>Culture is shared</u>: The last phrase in our working definition ---"as members of a society"---gives us another insight into the concept of culture, that is, that culture is <u>shared</u> among the members of a society. According to our definition, there can be no such thing as the culture of a hermit. In other words, there needs to be at least two people who share the things, ideas, and behaviors with one another. In actual fact, there are far more than just two people in any real world culture. But, irrespective of size, in order for a thing, idea, or behavior to be *cultural*, it must have a shared meaning among most of the people in the group.

It is this shared nature of culture that makes our lives relatively uncomplicated and predictable. To illustrate, when a businessperson from New York makes a circle with his thumb and forefinger, a colleague from Atlanta has no difficulty understanding that gesture as meaning "A-OK."

This is because both people share the cultural meaning attached to that gesture. But should the New Yorker make the same gesture to a potential customer in parts of South America, it would mean something very different (and offensive) because the two people do not have a shared cultural meaning for that gesture. Thus, the shared nature of culture becomes very evident when we step outside of our own safe cultural boundaries.

Culture is learned: People acquire their culture through the process of learning, not through their genes. To be certain, all humans have a wide variety of biologically based physical traits, such as stature, facial features, hair color and texture, blood type, and whether one has an attached or detached ear lobe, among many other characteristics. But you also have *cultural* traits, such as how you behave and how you think, which you acquire through the process of interacting with others in your cultural environment. Even though a child growing up in North Dakota learns many things that are different from those learned by a child in Brazil, the process of acquiring one's culture is the same. Since both children were born into already existing cultures, they had to learn how to think and behave from those around them, including their parents, siblings, teachers, priests, and playmates.

It is important to keep in mind that while all peoples of the world learn their cultures, the *content* of what is learned varies enormously between cultures. Just because a Hadza forager from Tanzania does not know how to operate a jet ski, we should not conclude that he is less intelligent than we are. There are many things that he has learned that we have not, such as how to track a wounded bushbuck, find water under the ground, and generally survive in an inhospitable environment. And he has learned these things every bit as efficiently as we have learned how to solve an algebraic equation. These people have simply learned different cultural content, which, in both cases, helps people adapt to their environments. There is no evidence to suggest that some cultures are faster or slower learners than others.

This insight that culture is <u>learned</u>, and not genetically transmitted, is important in our quest to become globally savvy. For example, the learned nature of culture should remind us that since we learned our own culture, it is certainly possible to learn someone else's culture. Conversely, the learned nature of culture suggests to us that even though your foreign workers do not have certain job-related skills now, they are perfectly capable of learning them in the future. And finally, if you believe that culture is learned, you will avoid the pitfall of concluding that culturally different people (because they do not know what you know) are congenitally stupid. This can only enhance tolerance for cultural differences, a prerequisite for success when conducting business in a global setting.

<u>Cultures are adaptive</u>: Culture represents the major way by which human populations adapt or relate to their environments so that they can continue to reproduce and survive. Most non-human organisms adapt to their environments by certain biological features that equip them to maximize their chances for survival. Predators such as wolves, lions, and leopards, for example, have developed powerful jaws and canine teeth used for killing animals and ripping their flesh. Humans, by way of contrast, have relied more on cultural than biological features for adapting to their environments. Through the use of such cultural tools as spears, arrows, guns, and knives, humans are able to kill and butcher animals even more efficiently than an animal could with its massive jaws and teeth. The discovery of such chemical substances as penicillin, quinine, and the polio vaccine has provided the human species a measure of protection against disease and death. The proliferation of agricultural technology over the past century has dramatically increased peoples' capacity to feed themselves. Because humans rely much more heavily on cultural adaptation than biological adaptation, they are enormously flexible in their ability to survive and thrive in a

wide variety of natural environments. Because of the adaptive nature of culture, people are now able to live in many previously uninhabitable places, such as deserts, the polar region, under the sea, and even in outer space.

The notion that culture is adaptive should not lead us to the conclusion that every aspect of a culture is adaptive. It is possible for some features to be adaptively neutral, neither enhancing nor diminishing the capacity of a people to survive. Moreover, it is even possible for some features of a culture to be maladaptive or dysfunctional. To illustrate, the large-scale use of automobiles coupled with industrial pollutants is currently destroying the quality of the air in our environment. If this set of cultural behaviors continues unchecked, it will destroy our environment to such an extent that it will be unfit for human habitation.

Cultures are always changing: As with just about everything else in the world, cultures don't remain unchanged, or at least not for long. Just look through a Sears and Roebuck catalogue of the 1960s to see how our material culture has changed. And our cultural ideas and behavior patterns have changed no less dramatically over the decades. Some cultures (those somewhat isolated from the global economy) may change more slowly than others, but all cultures of the world constantly have to deal with change.

Cultures change in two basic ways, from within and from outside of the society. Internal changes are brought about by innovations by creative members of the society. Oftentimes these innovations are only slight variations in what already exists in the society. To illustrate, the automobile was invented in Europe because it was part of a cultural traditional that already included the internal combustion engine and the horse-drawn carriage. Thus, invention frequently, but not always, involves the recombination of already-existing cultural items. The other source of cultural change is known as "cultural diffusion," that is, the spreading of things, ideas, and behaviors from one cultural to another. Since it is easier to borrow a cultural item than it is to invent it, cultural diffusion is responsible for the greatest amount of culture change.

Understanding this basic idea that cultures are constantly changing is important for the globally savvy player for a number of reasons. First, since all cultural environments are experiencing change, they are in constant need of monitoring. Products marketed to a particular foreign culture two decades ago might (owing to changing values) be very inappropriate in today's markets. Second, despite a lack of fit between a corporate culture and its foreign work force, the fact that cultures can, and do, change should remind us that whatever cultural gap exists can be minimized. And third, since cultural diffusion is a two-way process (borrowing takes place in both directions), the leader with global brains should be receptive to the idea that the corporate culture (in addition to the local culture) is capable of cultural borrowing. In fact, the local culture may have a good deal to offer the corporate culture, provided that those in the corporate culture are willing to accept it.

MAKING SENSE OF CULTURAL DIFFERENCES

Whenever encountering a new culture, either at home or abroad, you never encounter the whole culture at once. Rather, you run into bits and pieces of a culture at any given time. You might be faced with an unusual behavior, an idea, an attitude, or a thing, which requires your understanding. When this happens, there are essentially two ways to make sense out of this unfamiliar cultural element. The first way, and the method used by most people most of the time, is to examine the idea or behavior in terms of how it fits into your own culture. In other words, you try to make sense of this idea, which has just been expressed by your Nigerian coworker, within the context of your own cultural framework. In most situations this approach will not be very useful for increasing your understanding. This is because you have taken the Nigerian's idea from its original cultural context and attempted to analyze it in terms of a foreign cultural context, namely your own. This process of analyzing or evaluating parts of other peoples' culture in terms of your own is known as *ethnocentrism*. Inherent in the ethnocentric approach is that one's own culture is superior to all others. It is important to understand the ethnocentric approach to dealing with cultural differences because once you fully understand it, you can avoid ever using it again.

The concept of ethnocentrism can be illustrated by the following example. While waiting to cross the street in Bombay, India, an American tourist stood next to a local resident, who proceeded to blow his nose in the street. The tourist's reaction was instantaneous and unequivocal: "How disgusting!" he thought to himself. He responded to this cross-cultural encounter by evaluating the Indian man's behavior on the basis of standards of etiquette established by his own culture. According to those standards, it would be considered proper to use a handkerchief in such a situation. But if the man from Bombay saw the American tourist blowing his nose into a handkerchief, he would be equally repulsed. The Indian would think it strange for the man to blow his nose into a handkerchief and then put the handkerchief back into his pocket and carry it around for the rest of the day. Both the American and the Indian would be evaluating each other's behavior based on the standards of their own cultural assumptions and practices. In other words, both would be viewing the rest of the world through the narrow lens of their own culture.

The other, and by far the superior, way of understanding different cultures is to examine the idea or behavior in terms of its *original cultural context*. Before coming to any conclusions about the foreign cultural element, it is important to suspend judgement until you have more complete information about other parts of that culture. In other words, how does this particular foreign idea fit into its original cultural context? Armed with this contextual knowledge, I can virtually guarantee that the idea or behavior will begin to make sense to you. This approach of analyzing a cultural element from within its original context does not require you to adopt it as your own. In fact, you don't even have to like it. But if you want to *understand* why the Nigerian thinks or acts the way he does, you need to look at his ideas and behaviors in terms of *his* total culture, not yours.

Perhaps a specific example of these two approaches to cross-cultural understanding is in order. The traditional Inuit of Canada practice a custom that strikes most westerners as inhumane. When aging Inuit parents become too old to contribute labor to the household, they are left out on an ice flow to die. If we viewed this practice solely from the perspective of our own culture (that is, ethnocentrically), we would naturally conclude that it was cruel and heartless. How could any sane person allow his parents---the very people that brought him into the world---to freeze to death? But, when viewed from the perspective of the total Inuit culture, the practice tends to make sense. The natural environment in which traditional Inuit live is probably the most inhospitable in the world. If any member of the society cannot pull his or her own weight, the entire group will suffer. Moreover, as Freidl and Pheiffer (1977:331) have suggested, "this is an accepted practice for which people are adequately prepared throughout their lives, and not some type of treachery sprung upon an individual as a result of a criminal conspiracy." Thus, when viewed from the perspective of the total Inuit culture, this practice is both sensible and functional.

CONCLUSION:

During these days of tight budgets, an increasing number of people are asking the question: "Why do we need to know about the cultural dimension of our business enterprises?" Why do we need to know about what people in other parts of the world have, think, and do? There are, of course, a number of very appropriate responses to these questions. For example, the comparative study of cultures (both national and business cultures) serves as a valuable check on those of us who tend to generalize about "human nature" solely on observations from our own society. People frequently assume that there own ways of thinking and acting are unquestionably rational, natural, and thus, human. Yet, the comparative study of cultures conducted over the past century exposes us to the enormous variations in thinking and behaving found in the contemporary world---and the many different rational solutions people have come up with for solving the basic societal problems. Moreover, as I have argued elsewhere (Ferraro, 2001), the comparative study of cultures is eminently useful in today's world. Since all of us (whether we are architects, educators, businesspeople, administrators, or nurses) conduct our personal and professional lives within a cultural (or even multicultural) context, then cultural studies really do have something to offer those of us outside of the university classroom.

But, perhaps the most "bottom-line" reason for studying other cultures is that it contributes to self-knowledge. Thousand of years ago the Greeks claimed that to be educated involved "knowing yourself." There is no better way to acquire this "self-knowledge" than through the comparative study of other cultures. That is, before you can understand yourself, you must first understand your own culture and how it influences your thoughts and behaviors. And, of course, the only way to understand your own culture is to study other cultures.

Cross-cultural Quiz (Answers on page 201)

1. While on a two-year assignment in Bolivia, Mary Herbert was invited to dinner at the home of one of her male Bolivian colleagues. Wanting to express her gratitude, she brought the man's wife a dozen purple tulips. But, when

presenting the wife with the flowers, Mary noticed that both the husband and the wife looked surprised. After taking the flowers to the kitchen, Mary felt somewhat insulted because the flowers were never displayed, nor was she properly thanked for bringing them. How might you explain this uncomfortable situation?

2. Ted Grote was in charge of setting up his company's exhibit at a trade show in Hong Kong. As an inducement for visiting the exhibit, Ted and his two assistants gave away green baseball caps with the company's logo on the front. During the first day of the show, however, very few people visited Ted's exhibit. And those who did refused the free gift of a cap. How can you explain this unanticipated poor response at the trade show?

3. Bryan Robinson, a vice president for marketing for a California cosmetic company, has been sent by his company to France to select a new sales manager for the Paris area. After sitting through a sales presentation (which includes numerous historical and literary references) given by one of the leading candidates, Bryan wonders why this person has been so highly recommended. While trying to concentrate on the candidate's presentation, Bryan begins to wonder if the candidate is compensating for his lack of technical knowledge by including excessive literary and historical references. Could there be another, more reasonable, explanation?

CHAPTER 3

UNDERSTANDING VALUES

A nthropologists and other social scientists who study comparative cultures estimate that there are between five and six thousand separate and distinct cultures in the world today. That is an enormous amount of cultural variability. Since most people never master the cultural features of even one culture other than their own, it is not very likely that anyone will ever master <u>all</u> the facts about <u>all</u> of the world's cultures. In order to help us make sense out of this cultural diversity, we need some conceptual help. Fortunately, social scientists not only collect facts about the many cultures of the world, they also develop generalizations by examining their similarities and differences.

In this chapter, we will present a conceptual framework of value differences found in various parts of the world. By the term "values," we are referring to *those things found in all cultures that are expected or hoped for; they involve embedded assumptions about what is right or wrong, good or bad; and they involve a set of standards by which behavior is evaluated.*

This framework is designed to help you learn from your cross-cultural encounters by providing a way to understand the value preferences of people from different cultural groups. It will enable you to see how your cultural values compare to other cultures on a number of important dimensions. It will also provide you a set of "hooks" on which to hang (and better understand) the various culture traits that you may encounter in the future. This framework assumes that cross-cultural awareness will occur when you view other cultural values in relation to your own. And since cultural value differences lay behind breakdowns in cross-cultural communication, such a framework will help you diagnose, and avoid, miscommunications in the future.

This framework is designed to help you develop your own cultural self-awareness. Before it is possible to understand the internal structure and logic of another culture, it is essential to first understand your own culture and how it influences who you are and what you do. We are as much products of our culture as the Japanese, French, and Cubans are products of theirs. People from all cultures face a number of universal societal problems, from how to make decisions to how to help young people make the transition to responsible adulthood; from how to gain a livelihood to how to explain the unexplainable. How any particular culture solves these problems varies widely. Middle-class North Americans have worked out one set of cultural patterns, whereas the Indonesians have developed a quite different set of solutions. In most cases, one solution is probably not more inherently rational than another. They all represent different answers to similar societal problems. Yet, only after we understand why we do the things we do can we appreciate the internal logic of why other, culturally different people do what they do.

Any attempt to analyze North American values is bound to be a tricky business at best. Part of the difficulty stems from the inherent bias of analyzing one's own culture. Since we are all influenced, to some degree, by the experiences of our own culture, any attempt to describe that culture will inevitably be distorted. But equally problematic is the enormity of the task. Whenever we make descriptive statements about the nature of American culture, we are implying that there are other (non-American) cultures that possess the opposite traits. In other words, to say that people in the United States place a high value on the individual is to imply that there are other cultures, Tanzanians of eastern Africa, for example, that place a higher value on the group. Such comparative statements presuppose that we are dealing with two unified, monolithic cultures, that of the United States, on the one hand, and that of Tanzania on the other. In actual fact, the many cultures of the world cannot be sorted out into neat and tidy categories. Many of the "non-American" peoples that we tend to contrast with our own are linguistically and culturally heterogeneous. For example, in the country of Tanzania there are approximately 120 mutually unintelligible languages spoken. And, this level of linguistic heterogeneity brings with it an equal level of cultural variability as well.

Similarly, some would question the very legitimacy of referring to the American culture. Despite the often heard claims that the United States is a great "melting pot," many sub-cultural groups, particularly in major urban areas, have retained a good deal of their ethnic distinctiveness. There are, for example, appreciable numbers of Chicanos in Los Angeles, Arabs in Detroit, Japanese in Seattle, Chinese in San Francisco, and Italian-Americans in Boston, New York, Philadelphia, and Baltimore. In fact, over 60% of the people living in Miami do not speak English as their first language. According to the latest U.S. Census, there are approximately 20 million foreign-born people living in the United States and over 31 million (roughly 14 percent) who do not speak English as their primary language. As an indication of this considerable diversity, the United States is a country in which both the late Mother Teresa (a nun who ministered to the needs of the poor) and Madonna (the sexually explicit bad girl of popular music) appeared on the same list of "most admired women." Moreover, it is not unusual to observe at a Haitian street festival in NY City a Chinese woman eating a slice of pizza in front of a green grocery run by a Korean family. Owing to this cultural complexity, it might be more reasonable to think of the United States as less of a "melting pot" and more as a "salad bowl," whereby the individual sub-cultures retain their own identity and integrity.

While acknowledging the difficulties inherent in generalizing about values in such heterogeneous societies as Tanzania and the United States, some contrasting of value patterns certainly is possible. In fact, the dual processes of generalizing and comparing are imperative if we are to enhance our understanding of other cultures as well as our own. Whether we live in Massachusetts or California, Oregon or Florida, in a small town or a large metropolis, there are some common U.S. values that stop abruptly at the Rio Grande and somewhat less dramatically at the Canadian border. Over the last several centuries, the United States has woven together threads of culture from all over the world into a cultural tapestry that is quite distinct and recognizable. Owing to certain common experiences in their up-bringing, most Americans share a body of attitudes, values, beliefs, and behavior patterns. As Edward and Mildred Hall have suggested:

> You can pick out Americans any place in the world, often very quickly, because of their behavior. Among their most observable traits are openness, friendliness, informality, optimism, creativity, loudness, and vitality. (1990:140)

The approach to value differences taken in this book is based on the use of "ideal types"---broad sets of logically opposite traits that can be used to compare different cultures. Such an approach has a long and rich tradition in the social sciences, dating back to such 19th century theorists as Ferdinand Tonnies, Sir Henry Maine, Louis Henry Morgan, and Emile Durkheim. More recently, a number of 20th century scholars have used "ideal types" to describe fundamentally different types of social systems. These include the "value orientations" put forth by Florence Kluckhohn and her associates at Harvard (Kluckhohn &

Strodtbeck, 1961) and later applied to a cross-cultural business context by Hofstede (1980) and Hampden-Turner and Trompenaars (1993, 1998). This approach is predicated on the notion that people in all societies face certain universal problems, all of which have a limited number of solutions. To illustrate, all societies must somehow deal with the question of reckoning time. Some societies like our own take the precise reckoning of time very seriously by placing a high value on punctuality, deadlines, and not wasting time. Other societies have a much more loosely structured notion of reckoning time, whereby social relationships, not the arbitrary position of the hands of a clock, will determine when people should do something. However, all societies do not fall into one of two categories, those reckoning time precisely and those reckoning time loosely. Instead, we need to view these value orientations as *relative points on a continuum* rather than as two mutually exclusive categories. All cultures of the world, in other words, can be placed relative to one another along this time continuum, with some closer to the "precise polarity" and others more toward the "loose polarity."

When referring to the values of any specific cultural group, we are using "ideal types" to make large generaliza-tions of a comparative nature. No statement that we make about cultural values will be a perfect representation of reality, an absolutely precise description of cultural patterns. Some of the value traits we identify as "typically American" will be found, to some degree, in other cultures; moreover, there will be a number of people living in the United States who do not hold these cultural values. Our discussion of basic values is not intended to enable us to predict with absolute certainty how any person in a particular culture will behave. Rather, our discussion of values should be viewed as a series of statistical statements of probability designed to help us better understand ourselves in a comparative context.

The remainder of this chapter, and all of the next, will be devoted to looking at ten major dimensions of cultural values. Why ten? There are others, not included here, that could be discussed. But in the interest of time, and without compromising on breadth, these ten are the most relevant for global business. Each of the ten value dimensions will be introduced by a cross-cultural scenario, in which communication between people from two different cultures breaks down. Each dimension will then be discussed in terms of how it plays out in different cultures. And finally, the implications of each dimension for global business will be examined. As we will see, fundamental differences in cultural values can lead to misunderstandings, bad feelings, and even the demise of global business relationships.

I. INDIVIDUALISM-COLLECTIVISM

While managing a project for your company in Lima, Peru, you notice that one of your local employees is particularly intelligent, successful, and diligent. Thinking he would make a great addition to the home office in Philadelphia, you offer him a job. Even though your Peruvian employee would receive a promotion, a large salary increase, and paid living expenses, he declines your offer. You simply cannot understand why he would refuse such a generous offer.

All cultures must ask and answer the following question: To what extent should people pursue their own individual activities and agendas rather than contributing to the success and well-being of the larger group, such as family, neighborhood, clan, team, or company? Some cultures, such as the United States, Canada, Great Britain, and the Netherlands, place a high value on individualism. These cultures emphasize the worth and dignity of the individual over the group, independence rather than interdependence, and relatively few social obligations. People are expected to be self-reliant, show initiative, and promote their own careers and advancements up the social ladder. Other cultures, such as Guatemala, Peru, Japan, and Taiwan, tend to emphasize the larger group. These cultures encourage people to put the interest of the group above their own, maintain strong ties and obligations to groups members, and value long-term social relationships above short-term accomplishments. People are expected to show loyalty to, and support for, group members in exchange for protection and a sense of belonging. This continuum can be represented in the following way:

Collectivists	Individualists
Groups are major units of social perception	Individuals are major units of social perception
Explain others' behavior by group norms	Explain others' behavior by personal traits
Success attributed to help of group	Success attributed to own ability
Self defined in terms of group	Self defined as individual entity
Know more about others than self	Know more about self than others
Achievement for benefit of group	Achievement for one's own sake
In-group goal over personal goals	Personal goals over in-group goals
Values modesty	Values self-assuredness
Values interdependence	Values autonomy and independence
Fears ostracism	Fears dependence on others
Strong connections to a few groups	Casual connections to many groups
Many obligations to others	Few obligations to others
Harmony expected	Confrontation is acceptable
Relations are important	Task completion is important

Let us return to the scenario described above. The reason that you don't understand why your Peruvian colleague turned down your generous job offer was the result of a basic difference in your cultural values. In the United States, where the emphasis is on the individual rather than the group, a person is expected to make decisions based on what will be in his/her best interest. Your very competent Peruvian colleague, however, comes from a culture that tends to emphasize the wider group. In Peru, people tend to first consider the needs of their family or company before considering their own self-interest. Your offering a promotion and higher salary would not be the most compelling reason for taking a new position. Rather, your employee will think primarily about the interests of extended family members, many of whom probably would not want him/her to move to another part of the world. Next, the employee will consider the interests of the local company, which probably needs her/him to continue working in Lima. What is best for the individual is not always the prime factor in deciding to take a new job.

Of the many cultures found in the world today, it would be difficult to find one that would be any closer to the "individual" polarity than the United States. While the notion of individualism has been a western ideal for at least the past several hundred years, it has taken its most extreme form in the contemporary United States. In fact, most of the research during the last several decades consistently shows the United States at the extreme end of the individualism continuum. The value of individualism is deeply rooted in the American psyche. Most Americans start from the cultural assumption that the individual is supreme. It is generally held that the individual not only can, but should, shape his or her own destiny. Anything that might abridge our rights to think for ourselves or make our own decisions is considered morally reprehensible.

Since the founding fathers had fought against a centralized monarchy, they distrusted a strong unified government. Individuals are protected by the Bill of Rights against infringements upon their rights by the state, which is seen as an instrument for satisfying the needs of the individual. Americans highly value their individual freedoms---to express their ideas, to practice whatever religion they see fit, to assemble freely, and generally to control their own lives to as great an extent as possible.

Even though Americans are quick to cite their constitutional freedoms, many view government as a necessary evil. Many Americans see the various levels of government as being too large, overly obtrusive, and unnecessarily controlling. Given this view, it is not surprising that Americans have relatively little respect for politics or politicians. And in recent years, this generalized disrespect for government has been reflected in dwindling percentages of Americans who exercise their right to vote. Voter turnout for recent congressional elections has been between 45-50 percent as compared to about 80 percent for both France and Germany, 75 percent for Italy, and 86 percent for Sweden.

With the emphasis in America on the individual, the family tends to be *relatively* unimportant. Rather than devoting large amounts of time and emotional energy on the family (the *primary* group), most American tend to divide their time between family and a number of *secondary* groups, such as voluntary or professional associations. This is not to suggest that Americans do not value their family ties, for the family, in fact, remains the most important primary group in the United States. However, many different non-kinship based groups compete with the family for peoples' time. The pursuit of self-interests, as compared to family interests, has resulted in the truncation of family ties. The meaning of the term "family" in the United States has been reduced to its smallest possible unit, the nuclear family, comprised of parents and 2.2 children.

Part of the notion of individualism involves a high degree of independence and self-reliance. From an early age, children in the United States are encouraged to think and act independently by forming their own opinions, solving their own problems, and making their own decisions. When children ask their parents a question, it is likely that the child will be told to look it up in an encyclopedia or on the Internet. While non-Americans might interpret this parental response as a sign of disinterest in their children, the parents themselves would say they are trying to instill in their children a sense of independence, autonomy, and self-reliance. They would, no doubt, argue that such training to be self-sufficient is absolutely necessary if their children are to survive in a society that offers an endless number of choices, from the supermarket to the voting booth. Stewart and Bennett remind us how children are encouraged to exercise their independence at a very early age:

> It is early in the morning and the mother has placed her baby daughter, who is less than one year old, in her highchair and is preparing to give breakfast to the child. The mother selects two different kinds of baby cereal, each kind packaged in a box of distinctive color. The mother holds up a box in each hand before the child and encourages the small girl to select the one she wants. Before age one, the child has already learned to express her own preferences and make her own decisions, at least with regard to food. (1991:133)

This emphasis on independence can be seen in early childhood education in the United States. The very ecological layout of the elementary school classroom in the United States accentuates the individual over the group. American students generally sit at their own individual desks. When the American student finishes her assignment, she will raise her hand and take the assignment to the teacher. Students in more collectively oriented societies, however, are often grouped around large tables holding six or eight students, often have their own group name, identity, and symbols, and will turn in their assignments together as a group rather than each student doing it individually.

That U.S. culture tends to emphasize individuality can be seen in our love affair with the automobile. There are more than 175 million licensed drivers in the United States who travel 2.4 trillion miles per year on nearly four million miles of roads and highways. By standing at any busy intersection during rush hour, one will observe that most cars carry only one person, the driver. Public transportation, by and large, remains poorly developed and under-utilized. North Americans express their individuality by wanting to be fully mobile, capable of traveling in any direction they chose rather than being dependent on the routes and schedules of public buses, trains, or streetcars. Despite the negative effects of urban sprawl, air pollution, and highway congestion, most Americans are unwilling to give up the sense of independence and individualism that their automobiles afford them. In a recent article on America's love affair with the automobile, Yates captures the sense of independence felt by one New Yorker who commutes daily in his BMW from Westchester County to Manhattan:

> *It's the only time of the day when I'm alone and completely in control of my own destiny. It's egregiously expensive, considering the tolls and the parking, and heaven knows it can be slow and frustrating. But it's my choice, and . . . that's important.* (1996:14)

There is a fundamental belief in the United States that the individual should be able to pursue his or her own agenda with a minimum of interference by the state or any social group. When individuals are able to succeed through personal efforts---particularly when having to overcome obstacles in the process---they are held up as role models, given hero status, and praised for surmounting societal constraints. And, more often than not, the individual is likely to take credit for the success. Ironically, most Americans have difficulty taking responsibility when their efforts fall short of success. Whereas they attribute their successes to their own superior efforts, their failures are often explained away by circumstances beyond their own personal control. A person claims that his illiteracy is the result of poor teachers; or his murdering his neighbor was due to temporary insanity; or he is an alcoholic because of alcoholic genes.

American individualism carries with it the strong desire for privacy. People, in other words, need a certain amount of time to be away from other people. The high value placed on privacy in the United States can be better understood if we realize that in a number of societies in the world the concept of privacy either does not exist or, if it does, carries a negative connotation. American cultural anthropologist Russell Bernard describes a major problem he and his wife experienced while living and working in Greece:

> When we first went out to the island of Kalymnos in Greece in 1964, my wife and I rented quarters with a family. The idea was that we'd be better able to learn about family dynamics. Women of the household were annoyed and hurt when my wife asked for a little time to be alone. When I came home at the end of each day's work, I could never just go to my family's room, shut the door, and talk to my wife about my day, or hers, or our new baby's. If I didn't share everything during waking hours with the family we lived with, they felt rejected. After about two months of this, we finally had to move out and find a house of our own. . . . As it turns out, there is no word for the concept of privacy in Greek. The closest gloss translates as "being alone", and connotes loneliness. (1988:165-66)

Individualism is such an integral part of American culture that we often fail to recognize its pervasiveness. We can gain a fuller appreciation of how individualistic American culture is by looking at some cultures at the other end of the "individual-collective continuum." Just as individualism can be traced through the very fabric of American culture, the collective orientation can be seen influencing the thoughts and behaviors of certain non-American cultures. To illustrate, how people identify themselves will vary from culture to culture. When asked "Who are you?", most Americans would give their name (Tom Bradshaw), their profession (teacher), and where they come from (Pittsburgh). In answer to that same question asked of a rural Swazi man from southern African, he is likely to give his name, his father's name, and the name of his lineage (extended family), which may comprise 700 to 800 people. In Africa, then, one's personal identity is much more closely allied to the larger group, in this case the extended family.

While some property in the United States is held publicly, the norm is for people to control their own personal property, usually including homes and automobiles (frequently in conjunction with a bank), clothing, appliances, and other gadgets, such as televisions, stereos, and cameras. This notion of individual ownership of property carries with it the idea that individuals have primary, if not exclusive, rights and obligations to their personal property. They can use it, sell it, hoard it, squander it, or give it away. And they legally can go to considerable lengths to protect it. Even small children in the United States have strong property rights over certain things ("Kathryn, how often have I told you, that bike belongs to your brother?"). This notion of individual property rights, so characteristic of American culture, is in stark contrast with cultures at the other end of the property continuum in which the verb "to own" barely exists. This is because in some cultures most property is controlled by a larger group, such as the extended family. As I have stated elsewhere:

> *In many parts of Kenya, however, property rights for individuals tend to be much more limited and shared with other members of the group. To illustrate, in Swahili, the lingua franca of East Africa, there is no equivalent to the English verb to "own." If you want to express in Swahili that "Njoroge has a brown cow," you would have to use the expression "Njoroge ana ngombe," which means literally "Njoroge is with the brown cow." That is, he has the right to milk that brown cow at present, but tomorrow his father's brother's son may have milking rights. And next month that cow may be transferred to an entirely different extended family group as part of a marriage payment for one of Njoroge's male relatives. The decision as to who has these limited rights and obligations to any particular cow is made by the group, thereby making the disposition of property a collective decision rather than an individual one.* (Ferraro, 1998:92)

Basic life choices, such as what profession you will follow or whom you will marry, are decisions that are made essentially by individuals in the United States. Marriage, for example, is viewed in the United States as a highly personal contract between two consenting adults. In some other cultures, it is seen as a union between two large family groups. In these more group-oriented cultures, marriages frequently are arranged. Marriage negotiations are handled by family members of both the bride and the groom, and for all practical purposes, the choice of spouse is made by one's parents or other influential family members. In those cultures which still practice arranged marriage today, there is an assumption that marriage is much too significant a matter to be based on something as frivolous as physical attractiveness or romantic love. As anthropologist Serena Nanda reminds us, the practice of parents arranging marriages for their children in India is a serious matter that requires hard work and patience. Quoting one of her Indian informants, she writes:

> *This is serious business. If a mistake is made we have not only ruined the life of our son or daughter, but we have spoiled the reputation of our family as well. And, that will make it much harder for their brothers and sisters to get married.* (1992:142)

However, we do not have to look at cultures only in Kenya or India to find examples of cultures that are more corporate and less individualistic. The idea of a collective orientation, rather than an individualistic one, is well developed in Japan, a highly industrialized society with the second largest economy in the world. The Japanese are renown for their strong sense of responsibility to the group (country, family, or company). If individuals do not give their best efforts, they will be letting down the whole group. Both failure and success are team affairs in Japan. While examples of a collective orientation in Japan are numerous, one illustration is particularly revealing. In 1972, a Japanese terrorist went on a shooting rampage in the Tel Aviv airport, killing 24 and wounding many more. The world was stunned at such an act of brutality perpetrated at the hands of a Japanese, normally such tranquil, peaceful people. But what was perhaps ever more startling was the reaction of the Japanese government. Unlike most other governments---that would have expressed official condolences while denying any responsibility for the acts of any of its citizens---the Japanese Government sent a high-ranking member to make an official apology to the Israeli prime minister and then gave generous financial settlements to the families of the victims. This response is very much in keeping with the Japanese notion of responsibility of the group for the actions of any of its members. Group ties are frequently so strong that members feel a collective responsibility for the actions of any individual member.

The contrast between the individualism . (so characteristic of the United States) and collectivism (so characteristic of Japan) can be illustrated in their two different versions of a well-known childrens' story. Both cultures have as part of their tradition of children's literature the story of the "Three Little Pigs." In the American version, the first two pigs are eaten by the big, bad wolf, while the third pig, who had built his house of bricks rather than straw or twigs, outsmarts the wolf through his own individual craftiness. In the Japanese version, however, the first two pigs escape with their lives and join the third pig to *cooperatively* outwit the evil wolf. The moral of the American version is that the best individual will survive while the Japanese emphasize teamwork and working together.

Implications for Business: (When Dealing with Collectivist Societies)

1.   In highly individualistic societies, such as U.S. society, it makes sense to hold out incentives to individuals as a way of motivating them. But in more collectivist societies, such as Japan, one's primary responsibility is to one's work group, not one's own professional advancement. Thus, to single out an individual member of a Japanese work team for praise or reward is likely to embarrass the individual and demoralize the others on the team.

2.   Be aware of the need to build long-term relationships. If building long-term relationships is the only way to do business with people in collectivist societies, then Americans will need to spend time and energy nurturing these relationships.

3.   When dealing with people from collectivist societies, Americans need to develop patience because building the necessary relationships takes time and effort. Once the relationships have been established, however, there will be a greatly diminished role of lawyers and detailed legal contracts.

4.   Be careful about using the pronoun "I". Often Americans use the pronoun "I" much more frequently than they use the word "we." People from collectivist societies sometimes get the impression that Americans are "loose cannons" (John Wayne types, shooting from the hip), speaking for themselves rather than the organizations they represent.

5.   Expect that rules, policies, and procedures will be applied in a particularistic way rather than universally.

6.   Do not discount family, tribal, or national loyalties, for they may be much stronger than your own.

7.   Use third parties to make initial contacts and introductions (such as your country's embassy officials, official trade missions, or specialized consulting firms) that serve as liaisons with potential business partners.

8.   When dealing with collectivist societies, take extra precautions to safeguard intellectual properties (which are not taken as seriously as in more individualistic societies).

9.   Communicate respect for the wider good (i.e., environment, whole society) rather than simply the

good of the organization. Collectivist societies tend to be more publicly conscious.

10. Emphasize your own sense of loyalty and that of your company because loyalty and the meeting of obligations are important to people in collectivist societies.

II. DOING-BEING

You are working on a joint venture with a Mexican computer company. Some problems arise in production and you are requested to travel to Mexico City to work out the kinks. On the first day of the scheduled three days' worth of meetings, you are frustrated by the lack of progress and suggest that lunch be brought in so that the team can work through the lunch hour. The Mexicans reply that this is not possible. Since it is a day of fiesta (holiday), they are all leaving at 2:00 pm to attend an office party. You are furious that you flew all the way to Mexico City only to make a half-day of progress on the first day of meetings. In turn, your Mexican colleagues are quite surprised by your anger. What is going on here?

Another major value dimension that varies among the cultures of the world deals with the meaning of action. Toward one pole of the continuum are those cultures (e.g., Canada, the U.S., and Belgium) that are task-centered. They stress productive activity and highly reward achievement and accomplishment. Work is seen as good in and of itself, and in fact, people are often evaluated, and even defined, by what they do. At the other polarity are those cultures (e.g., Japan and most countries in South America) that emphasize social skills and inner traits as being more important than accomplishments. In these cultures people work to live, they don't live to work. While work is not unimportant, these cultures tend to stress the experience gained from working rather than the actual products of the work. Unlike the "doing" cultures, the "being" cultures place a higher value on contemplation, thinking, the development of strong personal traits, and the maintenance of social relationships. This dimension looks something like this:

Doing	Being
Task-centered	Relationship-centered
People live to work	People work to live
Work for the sake of work	Spirituality/thinking
Accomplishments valued	Personal traits valued

The scenario above should now come into clearer focus. In Mexico, work is considered a necessary evil because people have to make money to satisfy the needs of their families. However, Mexicans have no trouble putting a task off until tomorrow if it helps them maintain important social relationships, even if productivity suffers. Since Mexicans reserve a part of their lives for leisure and pleasure, many outsiders might incorrectly think they are lazy. In actual fact, they are hard-working people. For example, during the Mexican siesta, which takes place every afternoon from 2 pm until 4 pm, employees socialize by eating lunch with each other or with their families. However, Mexicans return to the office, often working until 8 pm or 9 pm.

Since arriving in the New World, Americans have always placed a strong emphasis on work, activity, and achievement. Today, as in the past, Americans have been known for their high levels of energy, their aversion to idleness, and their preference for the person of action over the person of ideas. Constant work was an absolute necessity if the early colonists were to survive the wilderness. But, we would be guilty of the most blatant form of environmental determinism if we suggested that the high value placed on work and accomplishment was the result of the harshness of frontier life. Most of the early colonists from Europe were already imbued with the value of work per se. This strong work ethic arose from the Protestant Reformation, which viewed work as a means to salvation.

The Protestant Ethic---so much a part of American culture---holds that people do not work for themselves alone. It is through work---or a "calling"---that people demonstrate their worth to both God and themselves. Thus, work had a theological dimension. The Protestant Ethic linked work and success with a state of grace and eternal salvation in the eyes of God. Martin Luther held that a person's highest duty was the conscientious discharge of his labor. John Calvin also gave positive sanctions to work, achievement, and activity. Calvinists felt that they had the duty to prove, during their living years, that they were among God's elected for entry into heaven. And, the doing of good work would insure their salvation. This Protestant notion that work is not only respectable, but actually virtuous, finds expression in such proverbs as "All work is noble," "Idleness is the mother of evil," and "To work is to pray."

A strong American work ethic should not be surprising if we realize that the United States is a country of immigrants. Our earliest ancestors, and most who came to this country as immigrants, left their familiar homelands for the sake of making a better life for themselves and their offspring. Immigrating to a new and unfamiliar country required initiative, a fair amount of risk, and the understanding that the better life they were seeking would only come about through hard work. The immigrants understood the need for hard work because they were, after all, working class people, not members of the aristocracy.

The early American settlers, having arrived in the New World with a strong sense of the Protestant Ethic, gave it new meaning as they worked to create a new nation. Work for its own sake was (and still is) heartily revered in the United States. It has even been suggested that one of the major sources of conflict between Northerners and Southerners in the Civil War revolved around different interpretations of the work ethic. Many Northerners viewed slavery as wrong not only because it held blacks in servitude against their will but also because Southern whites were seen as losing their virtue by insisting that others do their work for them. According to historian Arthur M. Schlesinger, "after the Civil War, General W. T. Sherman found public occasion to thank God that now at long last Southern whites would have "to earn an honest living'" (1970:107).

So, Americans, from their earliest days as a nation, have placed a high value on work, activity, and "getting the job done." We tend to pay the highest compliment to contemporary athletes when we say "What a great player--- He'll do it all for you." We even have a saying: "The difficult we can do immediately; the impossible will take a while longer." One businessperson (Brake et al, 1995:132) has recounted this "can-do" attitude when he first entered the business world in the United States. When his boss thought he was taking too much time to make a decision, he was told by the boss, "It doesn't matter what decision you make. The important thing is to be seen making a decision."

As we pointed out in the previous section on individualism, Americans tend to identify themselves as individuals rather than as members of a larger collective. A large part of that individual identity is defined by one's profession. In actual fact, one's profession is usually the second piece of information we give to people when introducing ourselves. After stating one's name, it is typical to be asked, "And what do you do (for a living)?" Once we know that a new acquaintance is a school teacher, a CPA, or an insurance salesman, we feel that we know a good deal about the person because we understand how they spend their time and perhaps what they value. In fact, many Americans have Anglo surnames that reflect, if not their own profession, then that of an ancestor, such as Baker, Cook, Miller, Smith, or Carpenter. To suggest that Americans "are what they do" is to over-emphasize the importance of work and occupation. Nevertheless, what a person does for a living, particularly among men, is a significant factor in personal identity and how many Americans feel about themselves. This connection between a person's occupation and identity is encapsulated in such American proverbs as "Your work expresses you more correctly than your tongue," or "Do your own work and know yourself."

The degree to which work activity is intertwined with personal identity becomes particularly meaningful when Americans loose their jobs or are forced to retire. In an attempt to become more globally competitive, many U.S. corporations during the 1990s have engaged in what they euphemistically call "down-sizing," the systematic reduction in jobs or the redefinition of existing ones. Whatever term we use, it has resulted in many Americans either losing their jobs or having to redefine (in some cases quite radically) their professions. In either situation, the result has been significant psychological disorientation. Until that person gets another job, or redefines his professional work life, he may suffer a noticeable loss of self-esteem, if not an identity crisis. Not only does the unemployed person lose his daily work routine, but he begins to feel useless or worthless because he is not "producing." This can have a powerful impact on anyone from a society---like that of the United States---that measures a person's worth in terms of how much he can accomplish or achieve.

Rags to riches stories, accomplished through hard work and perseverance, were extremely popular during the 19th and early 20th centuries---and to a certain extent remain popular today. Horatio Alger (1834-1899) wrote a series of popular books in which the hero overcame poverty and adversity to achieve fame and fortune. More recently, such movies as *Rocky* and *Men of Honor* have continued this American fascination with the rise of the underdog, who accomplishes great feats essentially through hard work and determination.

During the Great Depression in the 1930s, it was not unusual for Americans to work for a company for no salary. Since jobs in some professions were simply non-existent during the early years of the Depression, some people would offer to work for an employer even though the company had no job or capacity to pay wages. During these times when jobs were scarce, these Americans thought that it was preferable to work for no compensation whatsoever rather than to be doing nothing at all. By working, they were at least gaining valuable work experience, while at the same time maintaining their self-respect by being a productive member of society.

This same loss of self-worth is often experienced in the United States when a person retires. People who have worked at a particular job all their lives suffer significant losses of identity when they are forced to retire. As a way of restoring the self-worth of retirees, retirement homes or planned communities often build meaningful activities into their programming. In addition to purely recreational pursuits (golf or bridge), many retired Americans choose to engage in volunteer work, such as working in day care centers, homeless shelters, or hospitals. Such work by retirees tends to legitimize their leisure activities because, even though they are not receiving money, they are being productive.

Some have suggested that work in the United States is a "calling," for it takes on religious or sacred significance. Work is so strongly valued that leisure activities are frequently seen as an extension of a person's work. During the early 1990s, a popular beer commercial on television ("This Bud's for you") portrayed various people in work situations. Interestingly, they were only able to settle back, relax, and enjoy their cold glass of Budweiser beer *after* the cows had been rounded up, the work shift was over for the day, or the hard work of the game had been completed (Hess, Markson, and Stein, 1993:66).

Like any American value, the value placed on work and achievement can only be understood in a comparative context. Among some other cultures of the world, work---particularly physical labor---is not highly valued *in and of itself.* This is not to suggest that people in these contrastive cultures are not industrious. In fact, they may engage in more hard work per day than does the typical North American. But they work because it is a necessity for survival, not because they derive dignity or self-worth from the act of working. In fact, if given the choice, people from a number of other cultures would prefer that others work rather than themselves. They would prefer to spend their time visiting friends and relatives, talking, contemplating, engaging in the arts, and generally participating in group activities that tend to serve as relief from the tensions of work. Whereas American culture, with its emphasis on "doing," encourages the kind of activity that results in measurable accomplishments, some other cultures instead emphasize personality traits. That is, most frequently it is the intellectual, contemplative, generous, wise, or just person who is held in the highest esteem rather than the person who works hard and performs tangible accomplishments.

Some observers in recent decades have suggested that the work ethic in the United States may be on the decline. Some studies have shown that Americans, particularly younger adults, are beginning to place less emphasis on the acquisition of money as the major motivator for working. An increasing number of young adults are placing more emphasis on aspects of work other than financial reward, including collegiality, creative opportunities, job security, challenge, and a chance to learn new skills. This should in no way, however, lead us to conclude that Americans, either young or old, are getting lazy or losing their strong work ethic. According to Harvard economist Juliet Schor (1993), the average American worker today is working 163 more hours (that's four full weeks) per year than in 1970. Schor points out that American workers in the 1990s on average work a full eight weeks worth of hours more than the Germans. So, even though the American workplace has experienced a number of changes in the last quarter of the 20th century, the intrinsic value of work (for its own sake) remains alive and well in American culture.

Implications for Business (When Dealing with Being Societies)

1. Be sensitive to issues of job satisfaction; employees are more likely to be motivated by quality of life issues than physical rewards like salary increases.

2. Employees expect to be evaluated on such personal traits as trustworthiness and personal compatibility, not simply on their level of productivity.

3. Work gets done only after strong interpersonal relationships are built.

4. Be sure to communicate who you are as a person (your character, beliefs, and morals), rather than simply what you do for a living.

5. Let people know that you highly value your social networks (family, friends, membership in organizations, etc.) in your own culture.

6. Avoid trying to conduct business via telephone or the Internet. People from "Being Societies" appreciate a more personal, face-to-face approach.

7.   Spend time building and maintaining networks of influential intermediaries.

8.   Expect to spend a certain amount of time socializing and generally engaging in activities that do not feel like productive work.

9.   Take your time. Try not to rush into talking about your business at hand.

10.   Develop a long-term view of doing business, rather than simply making a deal or signing a contract.

III. EQUALITY-HIERARCHY

Eric Anderson is managing a distribution project in his company's plant in Nairobi, Kenya. Since he is faced with an important deadline, he asks his employees to work late. In an effort to have them respect his request, he tells them that he will work late with them to get the job done. However, after fifteen minutes of packing and lifting boxes, he notices that instead of being appreciative, his employees are being disrespectful. What did he do wrong?

This value dimension raises the question: How should people with different levels of power, prestige, and status interact with one another, equally or unequally? Those cultures that emphasize the equality polarity (such as Canada, Sweden, Australia, and the United States) tend to minimize power and status differences. Power tends to be more spread out among more people, people in higher positions can be questioned, and subordinates want their superiors to consult with them and be accessible. This egalitarian value orientation leads to relatively informal relations between people of high and low status, a general disregard of protocol, and a high level of delegation of authority. At the other end of the continuum (represented by such countries as Malaysia, Panama, and the Philippines) people expect that status and power hierarchies will be strictly maintained. In fact, hierarchical inequalities are viewed as essential for the society's well-being because it satisfies a need for structure, order, and security. People at the higher levels of the hierarchy are treated with great deference and respect by those lower down the ladder. People in authority should not step out of their privileged roles, bosses should not be questioned, and there is little or no delegation of authority. This dimension can be represented in the following way:

Equality	Hierarchy
Low status differences	High status differences
Power diffused to many people	Power concentrated with few people
Delegation of authority	Little delegation of authority
Informal social relations	Formal social relations
Minimum deference for superiors	Maximum deference for superiors
Jobs based on perceived ability	Jobs based on age or family affiliation
Subordinates expect to be consulted	Subordinates expect to be told
Superior can be questioned	Superior cannot be questioned
Little respect for old age	Great respect for old age
Mechanisms to redress grievances	No mechanisms to redress grievances

Eric's predicament in the above scenario should now come into somewhat sharper focus. In East Africa, as in many other parts of the world, status and rank are important elements of social and business relationships. In the United States, where people have a tendency to play down status differences, it is not unusual for the boss to roll up his or her sleeves and start working alongside those of lower rank and position. In fact, the boss in the United States is likely to become more popular by working (or at least making a token attempt to do so) alongside the workers, for its shows a true spirit of empathy and democracy. In Kenya, however, a boss doing manual labor is viewed as very inappropriate. It is believed that if those in high positions are not willing to maintain their dignity, high status and self-respect, it is unlikely that they will continue to receive the respect of their employees. To the African employees it would have been preferable to have missed the deadline than to have their boss lose his self-respect by engaging in manual labor.

The playing down of status differences, an important theme running through American culture, has its roots in our nation's early history. By moving onto the American frontier, the early settlers gave up much of the formality found in Europe. The hard work required for survival on the frontier was hardly conducive to the preservation of pomp and circumstance. As a result, early Americans developed much less formal customs of dress, speaking, etiquette, and interpersonal relationships than found among their European ancestors. To a large extent, this informality and reticence to "stand on ceremony" persist to the present time.

Americans, who are very purposeful about their casualness, assume that informality is a prerequisite for sincerity. They become uncomfortable when faced with the type of ceremony, tradition, and formalized social rules found more widely throughout Europe. Moreover, they are likely to feel uneasy when others treat them with too much deference and respect. Many Americans view the British (with their dukes, duchesses, and viscounts) as overly pompous and socially rigid.

This general aversion to social rank is so widespread that most Americans resist showing deference to those whose status is based on ascribed traits (e.g., age, birth). In fact, Americans generally take considerable delight when those in particularly high or powerful positions behave just like the everyday person on the street. For example, we are quite reassured when we see George W. Bush in his running shorts or wearing Levis on his Texas farm. Americans tend to increase their respect for the company president who mows his own lawn or is seen down on the factory floor mingling with the hourly wage earners. By way of contrast, it would be considered very inappropriate for business leaders or heads of state in some parts of the world to be seen engaging in such mundane activities. Has anyone ever seen Queen Elizabeth of England wearing jeans? Wouldn't we be shocked if we saw the Emperor of Japan in a jogging suit running through the streets of Tokyo? Unlike the United States, such countries as England and Japan place considerably greater importance on not blurring the social lines between people of high and low status.

Thus, social relationships in the United States tend to be horizontal because they are conducted among presumed equals. This theme of playing down status differences---and the extent to which it is not seen in some other cultures---was dramatically demonstrated to this writer several years ago. While walking across campus to class with an armload of books, I met five of my students, four of whom were local students and the fifth was from Nigeria. After greeting one another, the six of us started to walk together to class. But before I had taken more than two steps, the Nigerian student turned to me and asked if he could carry my load of books. I initially declined, but when he insisted, I relented and gave him the books to carry. Immediately, I noticed several of the American students roll their eyes and shake their heads disapprovingly. It became immediately apparent that the Americans felt that their Nigerian classmate was trying to "suck up" to me so as to get a better grade in the course than he might deserve.

When we arrived in class, we discussed with the rest of the class what had just occurred. The U.S. students admitted that they resented the offer to carry my books because the Nigerian was not playing fairly in the normal competition for good grades. When the Nigerian student heard this interpretation of his gesture, he was stunned that it had been so thoroughly misunderstood. He explained that he offered to carry my books out of a deep respect for my high status as a university professor. Professors in Nigeria have such high status that it would be demeaning for them to engage in such manual activity as carrying a load of books. He went on to explain that he was motivated by the desire to prevent me from "losing face" by engaging in physical labor, an activity reserved for lower status people. Thus, this Nigerian student was acting out of a radically different set of values from those found in the United States---which is one of the few countries in the world where it is not considered inappropriate for students to address their college professors by their first names.

That Americans tend to play down status distinctions is hardly to suggest that status distinctions do not exist. Even though the social boundaries of class in the United States are not rigidly drawn, great social inequalities nevertheless exist.   The United States is an excellent example of a class society, whereby considerable differences exist between the various segments (classes) in terms of wealth, power, and prestige. Sociologists have identified at least five distinct social classes, including upper, upper middle, lower middle, working, and lower. Each of these classes vary widely in terms of income, education, and occupation.

Clearly there are in the United States enormous status differences based on wealth, power, and prestige. While Americans, as a whole, control huge amounts of wealth, that wealth is very unevenly distributed. It has been estimated that the richest one percent of U.S. families control as much money as the bottom 90% of the population. At the time of this writing (2001), Bill Gates, the President of Microsoft, was worth $56 billion. (That is, he was a millionaire 56,000 times over!). At the other extreme, over 50 percent of the U.S. population cannot afford health insurance. These great disparities in wealth are almost always associated with similar inequalities in power and prestige. Americans hold tenaciously to the idea that, although all people are not equal, they all have the same *equality of opportunity* to be able to move from "rags to riches." Of course, sociological studies for decades have shown that there are serious limitations to the notion of an open class society in the U.S. in which people have unfettered upward mobility. Nevertheless, even though, in actuality, significant differences in wealth and social status exist in the United States, the cultural value is to pretend that they don't exist. Thus, the cultural value of equality persists in light of overwhelming social evidence to the contrary.

The persistence of the value on equality explains, at least in part, the relatively informal way that Americans address one another. For example, waiters in restaurants often introduce themselves by their first names ("Hi. My name is Tom, and I'll be your server this evening") and proceed to treat their customers in a very casual way. Those in high status positions also frequently use their first names when introducing themselves ("Good evening, I'm Richard Slater, mayor of this fine town."). People from more formal, hierarchical cultures are often stunned by the informality of American speech and terms of address. To illustrate, French anthropologist Herve Varenne recalls the difficulty he had addressing his professors by their first names, an accepted practice among his fellow graduate students at the University of Chicago:

> Like many who first arrived in the United States, I
> had problems with forms of address. I gagged on
> calling my professors "Paul," "Cliff," "David,"
> "Milton," and "Vic." My professors could only be

Friedrich," "Geertz," "Schneider," "Singer," and "Turner in reference. . .and "Professor. . ." in address. . . . If I overheard (students) address professors by their first names, I inferred a familiarity that amounted to a professional anointment; I instinctively assumed that they could do so only because they had already been told that they had passed all the exams that would certify them as "the best." It took me several years to realize that professors could let students address them by their first name, still give them an extremely hard time, and eventually fail them. (1993:31)

The U.S. cultural affinity for informality (and de-emphasizing status differences) is reflected in the structure of everyday language. Such Indo-European languages as French and German distinguish between the intimate *you* and the formal *you*. For example, the German "*du*" and French "*tu*" are used with intimates while "*sie*" and "*vous*" are used in more formal situations with non-intimates.   If we consider some oriental languages, we can observe fairly complex systems, which require the speaker to make choices that reflect the social status of the people being addressed. To illustrate, before a word can be uttered in the Javanese language (Indonesia), the speaker must choose between the plain, the fancy, or the elegant style. Moreover, Javanese can use special terms known as "honorifics," which allow the speaker to express minute gradations of social respect within these three styles. By way of contrast, the English language makes no such distinctions.

To be certain, North Americans seem to go out of their way to play down the importance of rank and status. But informality is also evident from the strong desire in the United States to establish friendships quickly by getting on a first name basis as soon as possible. Nor are most North Americans reticent to ask relatively personal questions of a new acquaintance. It is not at all unlikely that after being introduced to a total stranger a North American would ask such questions as "Where do you work?" or "How many children do you have?" or "What is your golf handicap?" Since we are a mobile population, it is important that we establish friendships quickly before moving on to a new location. Such "personal" questions are a convenient way of telescoping the process of getting acquainted by enabling people to find a common interest. As friendly a social mode as this may appear to be to most North Americans, people from more formal cultures see this barrage of questions as brash, impudent, and an invasion of privacy, for it imposes a degree of intimacy that has not yet been developed. North Americans, on the other hand, frequently view people from those cultures that disclose less as being distant, evasive, secretive, and unduly formal.

Although many social inequities exist in the United States, most middle-class Americans like to think of themselves as being largely egalitarian. That the United States tends to be closer to the egalitarian end of the spectrum can be better understood if we look at those societies that are closer to the hierarchical pole. While all societies have some level of social hierarchies, in few countries are they as important as in Japan, often referred to as a "vertical society." Social hierarchies are much more deliberate and purposeful in Japan than in the United States. According to the tenets of Confucianism, people should submit to superiors and elders. In Japan, children defer to parents, younger defers to older, women defer to men, employees defer to employers, students defer to teachers, sellers defer to buyers, and everyone defers to the Emperor. This fairly rigid social hierarchy dates back at least as far as the Togugawa Shogunate, which had a number of distinct caste-like components, including the Samurai, peasants, artisans, and traders in descending order. This highly stratified social structure of the Togugawa Shogunate was very reminiscent of the traditional caste distinctions in 20th century India.

A strong social hierarchy still exists in Japan today, although it is based on achieved criteria rather than ascribed ones. With the exception of the royal family, people are no longer born into positions of high status, for now they must work for their privileged statuses. However, even though social status in contemporary Japan has become more achieved, very real differences in terms of age and gender still exist today. To illustrate, in traditional days the head of the Japanese family was the first to eat the rice in the household, while other, less important people in the family were expected to eat cold rice. The term "hiya-meshi-kui" refers to cold-rice-eaters, a term used today to refer to someone in business or government who is not particularly important. (Mitsubishi Corporation, 1988:50). Social rank in contemporary Japan is displayed in a number of subtle ways, including the relative depth of the bow, clothing, seating positions at meetings, and certain linguistic honorifics. In a Japanese office, the type of chair a person sits in reveals his/her status. The chair that carries the highest social status is the one with armrests. Most of the rank and file workers sit in chairs without armrests. Social order for the Japanese depends on everyone knowing their relative ranking in the society and avoiding any behavior that would threaten that order. Proper order insures social harmony, which is a high priority for the Japanese. The reason that business cards (*meishi*) are so important in contemporary Japan is that they enable people who do not know one another to learn each other's relative status so they will know how to interact.

Implications   for   Business   (When   Dealing   with Hierarchical Societies):

1.   In egalitarian societies such as the United States, it is expected that high status people will play down their superior rank. But in more hierarchical societies, people need to know from the outset what your status

is so they will know how to interact with you in an appropriate fashion. Thus, communicate your status, authority, credentials, expertise, etc. clearly, but without arrogance or boasting.

2.   Don't impose equality on your hosts. In hierarchical societies it is not expected that all people will be treated democratically.

3.   The decision-making process takes longer in egalitarian societies where all levels are asked for input. In more hierarchical societies, decisions can be made more rapidly because some measure of consensus is not expected from all levels.

4.   To what extent should you honor/recognize/respect hierarchies? It is not particularly wise or productive for a manager from an egalitarian society to play down the organizational hierarchies in other countries.

5.   In hierarchical societies a boss does not appreciate having his decisions or judgments called into question. You exercise your democratic inclinations at your own peril.

6.   Pay attention to different levels of social status when dealing with people from hierarchical societies. Don't expect that lower status people in your organization can negotiate or conduct business with those of higher status in the hierarchical society.

7.   Don't assume that all people in a hierarchical society have equal access to information.

8.   Use high-status individuals as your agents, contacts, and intermediaries. Without these high-status con-

nections, foreigners are likely only to have access to low-level bureaucrats with no real power.

9. Expect that there will be a greater level of tension in everyday interactions between high- and low-status people (or between young and old or between men and women) in a hierarchical society than in a more egalitarian society.

10. Realize that subordinates in a hierarchical society expect to be closely supervised.

11. Expect that subordinates in a hierarchical society will more frequently smile and repress negative emotions.

IV. YOUTH-AGE

While working at your company's home office in Chicago, you are supervising a new employee, Daniel Mungai, from East Africa. Because he is far away from home and without his family, you and your wife invite him for Thanksgiving dinner with your extended family. However, shortly after Daniel arrived at your home, you notice that he keeps referring to your father (a recent retiree) as "old man." With each utterance of the term "old man," your father becomes increasingly annoyed. Finally, your father, in quite a stern voice, asks Daniel to stop calling him "old man." Daniel was startled and embarrassed, but really doesn't understand why your father doesn't like him. What advice would you give to Daniel and to your father?

A major contrast between different value systems involves the extent to which a culture emphasizes youthfulness or the experience that comes with age. In such technologically oriented societies as Canada and the United States, young people are held in higher esteem than are the aged. It is believed that the young are energetic, enthusiastic, resilient, and resourceful, all traits associated with high levels of productivity. As you advance in years it is widely held that you become tired, mentally rigid, out-dated (i.e., "old fashioned"), and generally less productive. Many older workers in the United States today are being given early retirement or are being "outplaced" in order to make way for the younger generation. By way of contrast, other societies value the experience and wisdom that comes with advancing years. In certain less-industrialized societies (in parts of Africa, Asia, and South America) older people are afforded the highest status because they are thought to be the wisest, most thoughtful, and most trustworthy. Even in such societies as Japan and rapidly industrializing China, the notion of respect for the elders is still very widely practiced. In such areas of the world that respect the old, you are not likely to find a particularly good market for hair products designed to "get the gray out." This "youth vs. age" dimension can be characterized in the following way:

Youth	Age
Youth = productivity	Elders = wisdom
Youth = new ideas	Elders = experience
Youth = future	Elders = trust

Now that we understand that different cultures define youth and advanced age in very different ways, we can better appreciate the cross-cultural miscommunication that occurred between Daniel and your father. According to Daniel's culture, the term "mzee" (translated "old man" or "elder") is a term of address that conveys the highest measure of respect. By referring to your father as "old man," Daniel actually was treating him, according to East African standards, with the greatest amount of deference and esteem. But, coming from a society that tends to glorify youth over advancing age, your father took the term "old man" to be an insult.

As a youth-oriented society, the United States extols the virtues of the young while devaluing, or at least ignoring, the old. We emphasize what is new and young by keeping up with new trends and desiring to surround ourselves with new things and youthful people. Advertising in the United States encourages this love affair with all things new. By touting products as being "new and improved," the implication is that all others are old and outdated, and, thus, untrustworthy. U.S. clothing manufacturers have convinced us for decades to discard perfectly functional clothing because it is out of style. We have become a "throwaway" society, discarding what we have in favor of next year's newer and better model. Some have suggested that this disposable mentality carries over into our social relationships, for our homes for the aged are filled with the discarded faces from previous years.

Has the United States always been a society that has idolized youth and dreaded the inevitable process of aging? We have images of an earlier America, which was kinder to its older citizens. During colonial times, the elders were more highly respected, perhaps even venerated, by the community at large. Young people sought the advice of their elders, who freely dispense the wisdom of their advanced years. As is the case with many non-industrialized societies, a person's status increases as he/she grows older.

This popular image of the pre-industrial past, however, does not fit neatly with an accurate reading of historical facts. Since 18th and 19th century America was largely an agriculturally based society, one's status in old age was determined largely by land ownership. Elders who also owned land were afforded great respect and deference, particularly by their children because of their control of land, the single most important resource. But the landless, those too old to work, widows who could not inherit property, and the older poor had low social status and were treated poorly. It would appear that much of whatever respect was given to the old in pre-industrial America was more the result of their property ownership rather than their advanced age per se. There was never a golden age for seniors during which the elders were afforded respect and high status. According to historian Carol Haber (1983:5), "for many individuals, even in colonial America, gray hair and wrinkles seemed reason for contempt instead of honor; their age alone was not deemed worthy of respect." Thus, while there may have been an ideal of veneration of the old in pre-industrial America, in practice the veneration was reserved for a relatively small number of elite men.

Whatever limited respect for elders may have existed in pre-industrial America, it has been eroded in the industrial and post-industrial eras. Nowhere is this more evident than in the language we use to refer to older people. Most of the terms we use (e.g., seniors, the elderly, the aged, retired persons, golden-agers, mature Americans, or senior citizens), while not highly offensive, are not particularly appreciated by our older population. And, of course, there are a number of words for older people that are downright negative, such as coot, geezer, codger, fogey, fuddy-duddy, biddy, old goat, or fossil. There really are no terms for old people that have an unambiguously positive connotation, for the simple reason that no one wants to admit that they are old.

Since there are few advantages to growing old in the United States, it is not surprising that people fear the thought of aging and go to considerable lengths to postpone some of its more obvious telltale signs. Americans spend hundreds of millions of dollars each year on products designed to keep us looking young. A wide variety of hair-coloring products are purchased each year to help prevent the graying process. We try to hide our loss of hair with chemical preparations, hair transplants, and wigs and toupees. We buy certain dish detergents that promise to keep hands looking young and many forms of skin creams that claim to prevent wrinkling. Plastic surgeons can now make us appear years younger by taking tucks in our skin or rearranging our anatomy. And, of course, we purchase running shoes, exercise machines, and health spa memberships in an effort to keep our bodies looking slim and trim, which is to say, youthful.

The generally negative value placed on growing old in the United States is due, in large part, to the belief that old age brings with it a number of problems. Empirical research has shown that the majority of Americans believe that the elderly must deal with loneliness, inadequate income, lack of geographic mobility, failing health, discrimination in employment, inadequate medical care, vulnerability to crime, and general rejection by the wider population. While these are all concerns to some older Americans, there is a very wide discrepancy between how the elderly and the non-elderly view these problems. According to a study by Speas and Obershain (1995), most people between the ages of 18-64 thought that the majority of elderly were facing the above mentioned problems. But when people over 65 were asked, a much smaller percentage identified these as problems. To illustrate, 61 percent of the general public said that most older people had inadequate health care, while only 11 percent of the people over 65 identified this as a problem for them personally. Even though things might not be as bad for the elderly as most people think, it in no way diminishes the generally negative beliefs that the general population have about growing old.

This bias against older people is no more evident than in the mass media, particularly television. During the 1960s, 1970s, and 1980s, television programs rarely showed elderly people in anything other than peripheral roles as grandparents, dottering old fools, or has-beens willing to dispense pithy sayings from bygone days. This is particularly true for women over forty. It is true that this is beginning to change because of the increasing number of older people in the population. In recent years, older actors and actresses have had their own prime time shows such as Angela Lansbury (Murder, She Wrote), Andy Griffith (Matlock), Beatrice Arthur (Golden Girls), and Dick Van Dyke

(Diagnosis Murder).   Nevertheless, older actors remain underrepresented or misrepresented. In fact, the seniors activist group, the Gray Panthers, sponsors the Media Watch Task Force, which identifies television programs that portray older people in an unrealistic or unflattering way. Moreover, TV advertising reflects this fascination with the young. Most ads revolve around youthful beauties, active athletes, or "20-30 something" professionals. Television commercial jobs for older actors seem to be limited to ads for vitamin supplements, laxatives, or denture adhesives.

That Americans should take a negative view of growing old is supported logically by many of the other deeply held American values. For example, a key American value discussed above is individuality, independence, and self-reliance. Relying on one's own resources is considered the key to both success and mental health. Yet the aging process, almost by definition, brings with it increasing dependency on a number of things, including a fixed retirement income, Social Security, adult children, government health programs, and institutionalized care givers, to mention a few. Moreover, many older Americans, having been forced to retire, are no longer in control of their own professional and financial destinies. Thus, most Americans fear, even loath, the aging process because it involves a continual struggle to maintain one's independence and control over one's own life.

The way that Americans view time (discussed in the next chapter) also tends to explain why Americans look at aging so negatively. In a society that deals with time so precisely, people are very conscious about how time moves so relentlessly. The American saying, "Time waits for no one" is a constant reminder that the clock is always ticking. This fact of life takes on even more poignant meaning as you grow older. According to Holmes and Holmes (1995:180),

The aged retired American has no alternative but to sit idly at home observing his or her superbly

accurate gold watch (which the company presented on retirement) tick off the minutes and the days the life insurance company tables maintain are remaining.

Furthermore, Americans are future-oriented. Youth is so highly valued in the United States because the future belongs to the young. Thus, it follows logically that in a future-oriented society like the United States those persons who are least valued--the old--are those with the least amount of future ahead of them. This is why there is such a strong taboo in the United States concerning talking about, and planning for, one's death. Being a future-oriented culture, Americans don't like to think that their future is limited. But death is the ultimate (and final) limitation on their future.

By way of contrast, in many other societies aging brings respect and honor. Older people are looked to as advisors whose opinions are highly valued because of their vast experience. In these predominantly non-industrialized areas of the world, where relatively few survive past middle age, the very survival to old age is in itself worthy of respect. In fact, in some societies making it to an old age is thought to be the reward for living a virtuous life. Moreover, since the older people have had the greatest amount of time to hone their knowledge, skills, and capacities, they remain useful as teachers for future generations. Thus, older people are viewed as being wise, thoughtful, and trustworthy. For example, Samoan society draws its leaders from among the oldest family members; the Sidamo of southwest Ethiopia and the Samburu of Kenya consider the promotion to "elder" (usually reached in one's fifties) to be the most important transition in life. And in North Burma older people are held in particularly high esteem since it is believed that longevity is the reward for living virtuously in a previous life. Similar examples of respect for age have been described in the traditional ethnographic literature from the Phillipines to rural Bolivia.

Even in such highly industrialized societies as Japan, the traditionally high value placed on aging remains strong. For most aspects of Japanese life, there is a proper way of proceeding, a proper ways of doing things, known as <u>kata</u>. Since these "proper ways of doing things" are ritualized and are associated with morality, then those who have been around the longest have had the greatest length of time to perfect proper technique. It is for this reason that younger people are expected to defer to older people. Although a younger man may be better educated or better able to do certain things, the younger man is nevertheless expected to show deference to the older man. Even today the aged in Japan enjoy a high status and are generally well-integrated into Japanese society. Certain linguistic conventions ("honorifics") are reserved only for the elders. In family settings, the elders are served first, are seated in the most revered positions, and have preference for being the first to take baths. Through special legislation, the Japanese government has declared certain old traditional artists and craftsmen to be "national treasures." There is even a national holiday, Respect for the Aged Day, celebrated on September 15.

To claim that America highly values youthfulness is hardly to suggest that it will remain that way forever. The high value placed on being young---while, at the same time, pushing the elderly to the fringes of society---is already beginning to change. And, it is likely to change quite dramatically during the first half of the 21st century. If we project current demographic trends into the next half-century, we see an America that has more grandparents than grandchildren. Owing to stunning advances in medical care, Americans are living appreciably longer. At the same time, the dramatic increase in the number of households with two wage earners has discouraged the number of large families. This demographic trend will be further accentuated by the existence of the large "baby boomer" generation (those Americans born immediately after WWII), who will be entering retirement during the first several decades of the new millenium. It has been estimated (Geewax, 1999) that by the year 2040, there will be four times as many retirees in the United States as there are people of college age. If this is the case, then American society will be transformed in a number of ways, including, of course, the way in which youth is idolized and elders are ignored.

Implications for Business (When Dealing with Age-oriented Societies)

1. Don't be surprised if you do not find younger people supervising older people.

2. Show proper deference to older employees, irrespective of your relative professional positions.

3. Refrain from making jokes about old people or the aging process because they will not be considered humorous.

4. Be careful when handing out promotions to younger employees because it can cause problems within the organization to promote younger people over older people.

5. The term "old man" is a term of respect, not a put-down.

6. Never send a younger person, no matter how competent, to negotiate with senior officials from a society that highly values age.

7. In advertising to such countries, do not portray older people as insignificant or incompetent.

V. TOUGH-TENDER

Rachel Beretta, an account executive with a Dallas-based firm, had spent the last seven months working on a joint venture project with Sven Carlson in the Stockholm office. Having completed the research phase of the project, they were ready to present the client (a Swedish shipping company) with their recommendations. Several weeks before the presentation, however, Sven informed Rachel that he would be taking paternity leave for six months so he could look after his 3 month-old son while his wife returned to her job. Since Rachel was relying on Sven's language and presentation skills for the up-coming presentation, she was quite disappointed that he would leave at this critical stage of the project. In fact, she thought that he was really very unprofessional for taking paternity leave in the first place. Is there any advice you could give Rachel to make her feel less resentful of Sven?

The next value dimension, which we will call tough vs. tender, helps people define success. Do people in a particular society define success in terms of high status, material accumulations, and well-rewarded jobs? Or do they define success in terms of less tangible rewards, such as quality time with friends and family, good working relationships, or opportunities for spiritual or personal growth? The dimension examines the extent to which a culture prefers achievement, assertiveness, power, competition, and material possessions on the one hand, or nurturing, social relationships, and cooperation on the other. Tough societies tend to define gender roles more rigidly than in tender societies. To illustrate, tough societies are more likely to restrict various occupations to a single gender, whereas in tender societies it would not be unusual to find female truck drivers and male house-husbands. Tough societies place a high value on doing, achieving external, measurable goals, and accomplishing one's objectives. Tender societies, on the other hand, emphasize affiliations, character, personal qualities, nurturing, the quality of life, and the maintenance of social relationships. At the workplace, people in tough societies are primarily interested in task accomplishments, while people from the tender end of the continuum are more concerned with issues of job satisfaction, such as relationships with superiors and peers, the work environment, and how interesting and challenging the job may be. The tough-tender dimension can be represented as follows:

Tough Societies	Tender Societies
High gender segregation	Little gender segregation
Gender inequality	Relative gender equality
Careers for males are mandatory	Male careers optional
Few women in powerful jobs	Women in powerful jobs
Accomplishments highly valued	Nurturing highly valued
Highly competitive	Highly cooperative
High level of job-related stress	Low level of job-related stress
Task-oriented	Relationship-oriented
Values combat	Values compromise
Bigger is better	Smaller is beautiful
Separates family and work	Concern for family life
Live to work	Work to live

Equipped with an understanding of the tough-tender value dimension, we are in a better position to appreciate Rachel's frustration with Sven. Clearly, Rachel comes from a tough culture, while Sven comes from a tender one.

Rachel's culture places a higher value on accomplishing the job-related task (making the presentation to the prospective joint venture partner), while Sven's culture places higher value on meeting family obligations. Neither Rachel nor Sven were acting inappropriately, given their cultural expectations. They were simply operating from two quite different sets of cultural assumptions. Unfortunately for Rachel, the timing of Sven's "paternity leave" was not particularly well-timed.

This dimension is one that has appeared in the literature in many different forms and using many different descriptors. Perhaps most prominent has been the discussion of Geert Hofstede (1980), who used the terms "masculine" and "feminine." Of the four value dimensions measured by Hofstede, his masculine/feminine distinction has proven to be the most problematic, in large part because it overstates the importance of gender. In fact, the use of these gender terms implies, either correctly or incorrectly, that women in whatever culture lean toward one polarity and men toward another. While gender roles are not insignificant, it is misleading to suggest by the use of these terms that gender is the only, or even major, aspect of this dimension. Thus, we use the terms "tough" and "tender" because they allow for a broader range of sub-dimensions than simply an emphasis on gender.

Those societies that score high on Hofstede's Masculinity Index, such as Austria, Italy, Japan, and Mexico, believe in achievement and ambition, judging people on the basis of their performances, and the right to display the material possessions one is able to acquire. People in tough cultures believe in ostentatious manliness and the capacity to be both assertive and decisive. The more tender societies at the other end of the spectrum (such as most Scandinavian countries and the Netherlands) are less interested in shows of manliness and more concerned with making life choices that will improve the quality of life, such as service to others and working with the less fortunate. It should come as no surprise that countries that scored high on Hofstede's masculinity scale have fewer women in the workforce, have only recently granted women the right to vote, and tend to be more tolerant of wife rape (Seager and Olson, 1986).

In terms of education, teachers in tough cultures reward and praise their best students because academic achievement is highly valued. Students in tough cultures are highly competitive, assertive, and task-oriented. Failure is seen as a major catastrophe. In more tender cultures, students are not praised for their accomplishments because cooperation with others is considered the most important goal. Male students strive to be accommodating and work to develop a sense of community and solidarity with their classmates. Friendships, obligations, and loyalty are all more highly valued than academic brilliance or accomplishments. And, courses in tender societies (which tend to be the same for both boys and girls) are selected because of their inherent interest rather than because they might lead to a better job.

Another dimension of toughness and tenderness involves relative levels of modesty. In tender societies, which place a high value on social harmony, people in general, and managers in particular, acknowledge personal success and accomplishments much less frequently than in tougher societies. It is generally thought in tender societies that noteworthy achievements in an organization are seldom due to the efforts of a single person. People tend to play down their own strengths and assets while praising those of others. Thus, people in tender societies view people from tougher societies as being excessively immodest because they tend to over-sell themselves.

The tough-tender dimension also involves how different cultures define the relationship between one's work life and one's family life. In tough cultures, the priorities of family and work life are kept as separate as possible. Corporations generally disregard the well-being of employees' families in their strategic planning. For example, employees typically are transferred without consideration of the disruptive effects on children's education or the workers' obligations to aging parents. In more tender societies, such as Sweden or Norway, these family issues are taken into consideration as part of the corporate decision-making process. Thus, in such cultures, the sanctity of family vacations is preserved at all costs, maternity and paternity leaves are generous, and expatriates are selected, at least in part, with an eye toward family responsibilities. In short, as Wilson (1996:11) has put it, in tender societies "the role of the employee as a family member is more clearly recognized and respected."

A major aspect of the tough-tender value dimension is the extent to which a society defines roles by gender. While it is true that all societies of the world define roles based on gender to some extent, some societies have more rigidly defined gender roles than others. When compared to some of the tender Scandinavian countries, the United States, at least according to the data presented by Hofstede, tends to be a moderately tough society. Working women in the United States are typically concentrated in certain lower paying jobs. To illustrate, more than 99 percent of all secretaries, day-care workers, and check-out clerks in the U.S. are women. Moreover, women make up 96 percent of all nurses, 83 percent of the librarians, and 71 percent of teachers. The story is the same at the high end of the spectrum. Women comprise only one percent of all CEOs, 6 percent of partners in law firms, and 8 percent of state and federal judges. In addition, men tend to hold most of the supervisory positions, even in those professions in which women predominate.

When this dimension is examined in terms of political behavior, we find that tender societies tend to be more permissive societies in which a welfare philosophy predominates. Environmental protection is given legislative priority over economic growth. Governments in tender societies spend relatively large sums of money on foreign aid projects for less-developed countries and relatively little on armaments. To illustrate, Denmark spends more than one percent of its GNP on foreign aid to poor countries, as compared to only .12 percent for the United States. Tender societies attempt to resolve international conflicts through negotiation and compromise rather than saber rattling or military shows of strength, which are more typical of tough societies. Women play a much more prominent role in government in tender societies, as reflected in the fact that 43% of national legislators in Sweden are women as compared to less than one percent in Morocco.

A number of researchers who have conducted comparative studies on both tough and tender cultures have found some interesting, if not unanticipated, correlations. For example, Anderson (1991:291-92) suggests that in those tender societies, in which masculinity and femininity are not rigidly defined, there are higher levels of self-esteem, social competence, and intellectual development for both men and women alike. Moreover, Buck (1984) found that males in tough cultures may be generally less healthy physically because they are not able to express their emotions as openly as are women. This internalizing of emotions (both negative and positive ones) leads to higher blood pressure and higher levels of stress. Buck's conclusion is supported by Hofstede (1980:281), who found higher levels of stress in those cultures that scored high on his masculinity index. And, examining the relationship between femininity and subjective well-being (i.e., happiness), Arrindell (1998) found that tender societies showed high levels of happiness provided they were wealthy countries; among poorer countries, it was the masculine societies that reported the highest levels of happiness.

Implications for Business: (When Dealing with Tender Societies)

1.   Be sensitive to gender issues and the expectation of greater gender equality.

2.   Don't assume that all people are motivated predominantly by material gain. When managing employees in a tender culture, understand that issues revolving around general working conditions, hours, vacation time may be more important than issues of salary.

3.   Be prepared for people and the government to be more interested in helping the underdog rather than helping the wealthy and powerful.

4.   The "hard sell' is likely to meet with less success than the "soft sell."

5.   Try to suppress your winner-take-all competitiveness. Don't be offended if people don't want to spend an evening with you playing Monopoly.

6.   Be aware that your marketing or management decisions may have a negative impact on the physical environment. Then do everything possible to prevent those negative effects from occurring.

7.   When negotiating with people from a tender society, it is always best to look for a win-win situation.

8.   Don't be fooled into thinking that men who are nurturing and supportive are necessarily weak.

9.   When conducting business of any type, be willing to spend time, demonstrate empathy, and build relationships.

10.   Don't be shocked to find women in important positions within the company or within government.

Cross-cultural Quiz (Answers on pages 201-202)

1. While managing a plant in South America, Arthur Manson noticed one of his foremen giving an employee incorrect instructions on the use of a machine. Feeling the need to correct the misinformation, Arthur intervened and explained to both the foreman and the employee how the machine should be operated. The next day the foreman resigned from the company. What did Arthur do wrong?

2. Victor Costas has been selected to work on a joint venture project in Japan. Wanting to make a good impression, Victor brought some small gifts for his Japanese business associates. Knowing that Japanese are avid golfers, Victor chose as presents several boxes of golf balls, each containing four balls. But when he presented his business partners with the boxes of golf balls, they seem embarrassed and not appreciative. What went wrong?

3. Joel Faircloth was sent on a month-long project with a client company in Colombia. To demonstrate his good intentions, Joel gave each of his three Colombian colleagues an expensive box of beautifully wrapped, imported chocolates. His colleagues, however, merely nod in appreciation, and put their gifts aside without ever opening them. In fact, after several weeks Joel became increasingly annoyed because they had never even thanked him for the chocolates. What can you tell Joel to make him feel better?

CHAPTER 4

CULTURAL VALUES REVISITED

In the previous chapter, we set out a comparative framework for analyzing cultural values. Specifically, we examined five value dimensions: individualism versus collectivism, doing versus being, equality versus hierarchy, youth versus age, and tough versus tender. After introducing each value dichotomy with a cross-cultural scenario, the values were discussed in terms of how they played themselves out in different cultures and in business. Finally, suggestions were offered for interacting successfully with culturally different business people.

In the present chapter, we will continue with this same format by exploring the last five dimensions. These include how different cultures deal with time, direct communication, flexibility, control over the environment, and competition.

I. PRECISE-LOOSE TIME

Scott Wilson, an insurance salesman from Los Angeles, had made a 10:30 a.m. appointment with Mr. Monsour, the owner of an electronics factory in Riyadh, Saudi Arabia. From the beginning, things did not go well for Scott. First, he was kept waiting until almost 11:00 am before he was ushered into Mr. Monsour's office. Then, during the course of the meeting, Mr. Monsour took several phone calls and was interrupted by his secretary on three different occasions. To add to Scott's sense of frustration, Mr. Monsour seemed more interested in engaging in meaningless small talk rather than dealing with the substantive issues concerning their business. How might you help Scott deal with his frustration?

(such as Switzerland, the United States, and Germany), see time as a tangible asset that must be used efficiently and not frittered away.   People are expected to make schedules, establish timetables, and meet deadlines. Punctuality in such societies is highly valued. At the opposite end of the continuum, in such places as Africa, the Middle East, and South America, people take a more relaxed approach to time. Schedules and deadlines are viewed more as expressions of intent rather than as strict obligations. Instead of reacting to the arbitrary position of the hands on a clock, people are more likely to respond to social relationships that are occurring at the moment. People from cultures with relaxed notions of time see those who take time very seriously as being very rude because they are willing to cut off social relationships for the sake of keeping their next appointment. This time dimension can be envisioned in the following way:

Precise Reckoning	Loose Reckoning
Punctuality	Little punctuality
Rigid schedules	Loose schedules
Time is scarce commodity	Time is plentiful
"Time is money"	Social relations

Scott's frustrations from the preceding scenario should now come into clearer focus. Saudis do not divide up their time in the same way that North Americans do. Time is dealt with more flexibly. Scott would be well-advised to be more patient and allow more time when conducting business affairs in Saudi Arabia than he would in the United States. Moreover, what Scott considered to be "small talk" is a very important part of the process of doing business in Saudi Arabia. Trust is an important ingredient in business affairs. Before conducting business, most Saudis want time to get to know their potential business partners. They feel that there is no better way to do this than to socialize and get to know one another.

Time is a major concern for the typical North American. The majority of adults in the United States do not leave the house without that little gadget strapped to their wrist that tells them, to within seconds, exactly what time it is. We keep very accurate records of how much time we put in at the office because that determines how much we get paid at the end of the month. We measure how long it takes a breaststroker to swim 100 meters in hundredths of a second. Even our eating patterns, to a large degree, are influenced by the clock, for we often eat because it is "time to eat."

Unlike Americans, there are some peoples of the world that see no particular worth in punctuality for its own sake. Rather than doing something or not doing something because of a clock, their actions are prompted by seasonal requirements, the amount of daylight available, or social events, such as meeting one's obligations to close kin, friends, or business associates. In the United States, we normally eat our meals at certain times of the day because it is "breakfast time," "lunch time," or "dinner time." But in some parts of the world, partaking of food is determined not by the arbitrary hands of the clock, but rather by having someone with whom to share food. In fact, many non-western peoples interpret the American obsession with time as antithetical to meaningful social relations. North Americans often are seen as wanting to rush through their personal encounters so they can move to the next item on their agendas. This rigid adherence to schedules---which emphasizes punctuality over social relationships---is thought to be rude and dehumanizing.

For the American, time is seen as being fixed in nature, just another part of our environment, and as such is treated like a tangible commodity. Much like money, time can be saved, spent, or wasted. In the United States, the relationship between time and money is expressed in the idiom, "time *is* money." Since time is seen as a limited commodity, Americans want to use it as wisely as possible. When traveling, we use our time as productively as possible by bringing our laptops on the plane with us or listening to informational audiotapes in our cars. In order to save time, we rely on take-out food from fast-food restaurants or pop frozen dinners into the microwave. Many Americans want to continually upgrade their personal computers so they can save fractions of a second when retrieving data. In fact, the enormous proliferation of personal computers in the United States today is a reflection, at least in part, of the typical American's desire to save time by working more efficiently.

Just how serious Americans are about saving time is illustrated by a true story related to this author by a friend from New York City. During the December holidays, the New Yorker found herself waiting in line at the fresh fish counter of a crowded Manhattan specialty food store. She knew she was in for a long wait because her number at the counter was #132 and they had just called #47. However, after about five minutes she was approached by a fairly seedy looking man who asked her, "Hey lady, interested in buying #55 for $25.00? How about #74 for $15.00?" She couldn't believe it. The guy was scalping tickets at the fish counter! After turning him down, the scalper actually sold #55 for $25.00 to a well-dressed gentleman in an overcoat. After making the sale, the scalper turned to the women, shrugged his shoulders, and said, "Hey, time is money."

The American pastime of baseball would seem to be the exception to the rule. In the United States, time waits for no one. Despite the fact that most Americans these days think in terms of nanoseconds, baseball is played at a very slow pace. There is no clock. Normally a game lasts a full nine innings, which may take between two and three hours. If the game is tied at the end of regulation play, it can go on until someone wins. To watch baseball requires a willingness to suspend our usual obsession with the clock.

Owing to the very precise way in which Americans deal with time, promptness is highly valued. To be kept waiting, particularly for a professional appointment, is generally taken as an insult because it devalues your time. If

Americans are even five minutes late for a prearranged meeting, they are expected to offer an apology. If one is to be   fifteen minutes late, a telephone call announcing the delay is expected. The issue of promptness becomes particularly problematic when Americans are attempting to operate abroad. To be kept waiting thirty minutes for an appointment (as was Scott Wilson in the opening scenario) may be an extreme affront to the North American. Yet, for many South Americans and Middle Easterners, such a delay would be well within the acceptable range of tardiness.

This basic American way of dealing with time, compared to Cuban   culture, is humorously depicted by columnist Dave Barry (1988:3):

If a (middle class North American) wedding is scheduled to start at 2 pm Saturday, the wedding march will start at 2 pm sharp, and the bride will come down the aisle at 2:03 pm, no matter what, even if the originally scheduled groom has bailed out and the bride has to use an emergency backup groom taken right off the street.   In a typical Cuban wedding, the phrase "2 pm." is translated as "possibly this weekend." (True fact: I once went to a wedding at a Cuban home; I arrived 20 minutes before the scheduled start, and was greeted at the door by the bride, who was still in curlers.)

This obsession with time in America certainly influences the pace of life. Many non-American visitors to the United States often comment on how fast things happen and how rapidly people do things. Even though most people from all cultures understand the meaning of clock time (hours and minutes), each culture has its own vocabulary of time. In an interesting multinational study of time, Levine and Wolff (1985) compare the pace of life in six cultures (England, Indonesia, Italy, Japan, Taiwan, and the United States) by using some creative unobtrusive measures: (1) the accuracy of bank clocks, (2) the average length of time it took pedestrians on a clear day to walk 100 feet on a city street during business hours, and (3) the average length of time it took to buy a single stamp from a postal clerk. The findings suggest considerable cross-cultural differences on these three time indicators. A quick pace of life and concern for speed and accuracy were most noticeable in Japan, followed closely by the United States, whereas Indonesia scored consistently at the other extreme, followed by Italy.

By distinguishing between the exact reckoning of time in America and the more loose definition of time found in some other cultures, we are not implying that one is any better than the other. To be certain, Americans' concern with time and efficiency has led to the development of the world's most affluent economy. But, oftentimes Americans are seen by outsiders as insensitive and unfeeling robots so enslaved by the clock that they fail to enjoy life. They are simply so busy saving time that they never get around to using any of that saved time to smell the roses. This point was driven home to this author several years ago while vacationing in Italy. As my family was preparing to leave our hotel on the Italian Riviera, I asked the concierge how long it should take us to drive to Bergamo, our next destination. I was taken aback by his typically Italian response: "What difference does it make?" The Italian concierge just could not understand why I was so concerned about the number of hours and minutes it would take to drive to Bergamo. After all, I was on vacation, and to him, the most important things was that I enjoyed the trip, not that I made it in record time.

In addition to being very conscious about not wanting to waste time, Americans are what Edward Hall (1983:41-54) calls "monochronic." By this Hall means that Americans prefer to do one thing at a time as compared to some other cultures that tend to be "polychronic," preferring to do many things at the same time. Americans conceive of time in a linear fashion whereby they divide time into segments, schedule it, and put it into discrete compartments. This is best represented by the typical American's "day planner," where days are divided into 15-minute segments. We fill in these time slots with appointments or "things to do." These schedules---particularly if they are written in ink rather than pencil---are given top priority and should be altered only for the most serious of reasons. So, most Americans expect that if they have an appointment from 10:00-11:00 am with a client, that meeting will start at 10:00 am, will not be interrupted by other business, and will end by 11:00 am in order to be on time for their next appointment. Everything for the American is to be very tidy, timely, and focused on a single task.

The differences between those who are sequentially oriented (monochronic) and those who are synchronically oriented (polychronic) can be summarized as follows:

Monochronic Time	Polychronic Time
One task at a time	Multiple tasks at a time
Concentration on task	Easily distracted
Schedules taken seriously	Schedules not serious
Many short-term relationships	Long-term relationships
Time is a threat	Time is a friend

Once we understand this fundamental distinction between monochronic and polychronic, Scott's frustrations from the opening scenario should be more understandable. Saudis do not divide up their time in the same way that North Americans do. Since Saudis tend to be very polychronic, they have no difficulty doing a number of things at the same time, such as meeting with Scott, taking telephone calls, and having people walk into the office to ask questions. Moreover, polychronic people have no difficulty changing schedules at the last minute. This, of course, drives monochronic Americans crazy because they view this type of behavior as irresponsible.

It is likely that in polychronic systems there will be numerous interruptions. A business meeting may be interrupted for ten minutes while one of the partners stops to talk to an uncle that dropped by unannounced. The personnel manager will take telephone calls while interviewing a job applicant. If the phone rings while walking out the door, a polychronic person will routinely answer it rather than letting the caller leave a voice mail message. People living in polychronic cultures have elaborate social networks (involving friends, relatives, clients, and business colleagues) that must be nurtured and maintained. Consequently, these social relationships take precedence over schedules and deadlines.

Edward Hall illustrates the difficulties that can arise when Americans deal with polychronic people.

> *If a monochronic woman has a polychronic hairdresser, there will inevitably be problems, even if she has a regular appointment and is scheduled at the same time each week. The hairdresser (following his or her own pattern) will inevitably feel compelled to "squeeze people in." The regular (American) customer, who has scheduled her time very carefully, is kept waiting and feels put down, angry, and frustrated. The hairdresser is also in a bind because if he does not accommodate his relative or friend regardless of the schedule, the result is endless repercussions within his family circle. Not only must he give preferential treatment to relatives, but. . .the more important the customer or business that is disrupted, the more reassured the hairdresser's polychronic Aunt Nell will feel (1983:51).*

People in monochronic societies would argue that proceeding in a straight line is reasonable because it is orderly, efficient, and involves a minimum of effort. However, this type of straight line thinking may not always be the best way of doing something, for it is blind to certain efficiencies of shared activities and interconnections.

Sometimes juggling a number of different tasks at the same time may, in fact, be the most time-efficient. Using a butcher shop analogy, Trompenaars and Hampden-Turner (1998:126) cite the example of the shop in Italy (a more synchronically oriented society) where the butcher unwraps and slices an order of salami for one customers and then yells out "Anyone want salami before I re-wrap it?" Even though each customer is not served in order, the whole process is more efficient because it involves far less unwrapping and re-wrapping of the various types of meats.

Thus, the polychronic person conducts a number of activities in parallel without being thrown off his or her rhythm. By way of contrast, monochronic people envision a crucial path from which they do not want to deviate. Both approaches to time are usually so well ingrained in people that a person of one style will have difficulty when interacting with a person accustomed to the opposite style. To illustrate, a New Yorker is likely to think a sales clerk in Buenos Aires is extraordinarily rude when she is writing up his sales order while talking on the phone, drinking a Diet Coke, and flirting with another customer. Someone from a more synchronically oriented society, however, will think that his American colleague (who is talking on the phone) is rude because the American does not greet him when entering his office. To a synchronically oriented individual, it is considered a serious slight not to be greeted even while still talking on the phone.

Implications for Business: (When Doing Business with Loose/Polychronic Societies)

1. Suppress the urge to get things done quickly (because "time is money"). Instead, build relationships.
2. Suppress your impatience. You may be viewed as someone who wants to cheat his business partners.

3. Become more flexible in your scheduling and broaden your concept of what is an acceptable range of tardiness.

4. If you need something completed by November 1, then get your loose-time business associates to agree to have it completed by October 1 or even September 15.

5. Be aware that high-status people can keep lower-status people waiting, but the opposite is not true.

6. When meeting with an associate from a loose-time society, bring along paper work so you get some work done while you are kept waiting in the reception area.

7. Accept the fact that some foreign business associates do more than one thing at a time. Be prepared to be in several different conversations at the same time.

II. DIRECT-INDIRECT

Phil Baker, marketing vice president for a Texas-based computer company, was making a sales presentation to a potential client in Tokyo. Phil had just proposed what he considered to be a fair price for a large shipment of his company's latest version of accounting software. Much to his amazement, the three Japanese executives did not respond immediately, but rather sat across the table with their hands folded and their eyes cast downward, saying nothing. Fifteen seconds passed, then 30, and still no response. Finally, after nearly a minute of silence, Phil became so exasperated that he said with a good deal of irritation in his voice. "Would you like for me to repeat the offer?" From that point onward the talks were stalled and Phil never did successfully negotiate a contract for his computers. Why was Phil's reaction inappropriate and counterproductive?

Cultures vary in terms of how explicitly they send and receive verbal messages. In the United States, for example, effective verbal communication is expected to be explicit, direct, and unambiguous. Good communicators are supposed to say what they mean as precisely and straightforwardly as possible. Americans like to "tell it like it is," put their "cards on the table," and avoid "beating around the bush." A high value is placed on words, and in fact, a primary function of speech is to use words, logic, and ideas to persuade others to your position. Communication style in some other cultures, by way of comparison, is considerably more ambiguous, inexact, and implicit. In cultures such as Japan or Thailand, where less emphasis is placed on words, people rely instead on hidden cues, such as nonverbal behavior and social context. These indirect cultures have many different ways of saying "no" without actually having to utter the word. Moreover, it is not unusual for people from such indirect cultures to leave sentences unfinished or to tolerate intermittent periods of silence.

The Japanese have great difficulty saying "no." Instead of saying "no" in a direct, unequivocal way, the Japanese are more likely to give a conditional response, an irrelevant tangential response, ask a counter-question, change the subject, leave the room, or say nothing at all. Of all the indirect ways that the Japanese have for saying "no," silence is the most difficult for North Americans to handle gracefully. North Americans place such importance on words that the absence of words becomes very disorienting. Because most North Americans feel that silence is inherently unnatural, they frequently say things that get them into trouble in their haste to fill the silence. Phil would have been better off to have waited out the silence and then come back with another proposal or a question that would have kept the discussions on track.

The direct-indirect dimension of communication provides another important tool for understanding cultural differences in a global context. Indirect cultures use shortened phrases and sentences and rely heavily on implicit, contextual cues. Direct cultures, on the other hand, emphasize elaborate verbal amplification and place little importance on nonverbal or other contextual cues. Thus, this direct vs. indirect dimension of comparative values can be represented as follows:

Direct Communication	Indirect Communication
Explicit messages	Implicit messages
Confrontational	Avoids confrontation
Abhors silence	Silence is valuable
Risks conflict	Avoids conflict
Many words	Few words
In your face	Need to "save face"
Emphasis on speaking	Emphasis on listening

As would be predicted, direct cultures, relying on elaborated verbal codes, demonstrate high value and positive attitudes toward words. The Western world (northern Europe and the United States, specifically) has had a long tradition of rhetoric, a tradition that places central importance on the delivery of verbal messages. The primary purpose of speech in this tradition is to express one's ideas and thoughts as clearly, logically, and persuasively as possible, so the speaker can be fully recognized for influencing others. In contrast, in such indirect cultures as Japan and China, verbal messages, although important, are only a part of the total communication context. It is not that words are unimportant in Eastern cultures, but rather that the words are inseparably interrelated to social relationships, politics, and morality. Given this more holistic approach, the purpose of communication in many Eastern cultures is not to enhance the speaker's individuality through the powerful use of words, but rather to promote harmony and social integration. In such societies, one is expected to be sensitive to subtle contextual cues and to not assume that critical information will always be verbalized. For example, an American corporate manager would most likely ask a subordinate directly for the budgetary reports she needed as soon as possible. In a less explicit culture, however, the same message might be conveyed non-verbally by raising her eyebrow while glancing at him during a meeting at which budgetary reports were being discussed.

This cautious indirect approach, which suppresses negative messages, tends to wear on the patience of most westerners. While Americans often interpret this indirect style as sneaky and devious, it is, in fact, derived from the notion of "face," the public self-image that people want to preserve. That is, an indirect style is the result of a predominant concern to allow the other person to "save face." This preoccupation with saving face, at least in Asians societies, has its origins in Confucianism, which teaches consideration for others and concern for proper social relationships. In Japanese culture, "defending face" is a major factor influencing behavior, and the Japanese have developed a number of strategies for "saving face" or avoiding shame. These include *mediation* (using a third party as a go-between), *refraction* (statements intended for person A are made to person B while person A is listening), and *delegation* (portraying oneself as a messenger for another in order to state one's own opinion).

As a result, politeness and the desire to avoid embarrassment often take precedence over the truth. This approach, at least in part, explains why Eastern cultures have so many nonverbal ways of saying "no" without directly or unambiguously uttering the word. This practice has caused considerable misunderstanding when North Americans try to communicate with Japanese. To illustrate, the Japanese in everyday conversation frequently use the word *hai* ("yes") to convey not agreement necessarily, but rather that they understand what is being said. Moreover, when negotiating with Asians, it is important to understand that "yes" is not always an affirmative response. Before taking "yes" for an answer, one must ascertain if, in fact, it was merely a polite response that really meant "no." Asian businesspersons, for example, are not likely to say "no" directly to a proposal, but rather will reply in ways that are synonymous with "no."

This difference in linguistic style between direct and indirect communicators can certainly cause problems of miscommunication in international business dealings, even when the discussions are in the same language. Direct communicators, such as Americans and Germans, will select their words with utmost care because they want to be as clear and unambiguous as possible. People from indirect cultures, such as the Chinese and Japanese, also will choose their words with great care, but for different reasons. Their meticulous choice of words stems from their desire to avoid rude bluntness that can cause others to "lose face." Given these two very contrasting linguistic styles, it should come as no surprise that the meaning of the term "sincerity" has two very different meanings. In societies that communicate directly, the sincere person tells the unvarnished truth, even when it is not pleasant. In more indirect societies, on the other hand, the sincere person is the one who says he will help others, even though he knows that it is impossible.

This indirect style of communication found among the Japanese can be illustrated by two people, one American and one Japanese, wanting to buy a gold bracelet at a jewelry store for about $500. If they are shown a bracelet selling for $1200, the American is likely to say, "No, that is simply too expensive---I don't want to spend that much money." The Japanese, on the other hand, is likely to say, "I am overcome with admiration for this bracelet." He is every bit as committed to not buying the bracelet, but he is letting the salesperson down gently.

Nowhere is this direct-indirect dichotomy between Americans and Japanese more apparent than in television commercials. In the United States, we routinely encounter "hard sell" television commercials. The product being advertised is prominently displayed, facts are presented as to why the viewer should purchase the product, and a barrage of words is used to drive home the point. We are told that "Seven out of ten doctors agree. . ." or that "studies at a leading university confirm. . ." that Burpomatic brand antacid works twice as fast to relieve gas as other leading brands.   Or, we are likely to hear a very fast-talking announcer try to convince the viewer to buy a particular brand of automobile at this weekend's gigantic sale-a-thon, and, to enhance the sense of excitement, he will literally shout the words into the camera at hyper-speed.

Such a direct, no-nonsense, take-no-prisioners approach to marketing is in stark contrast to the typical Japanese commercial, which tends to be artistically filmed but very indirect in approach. They do not preach, coerce, promise, or even praise their products. In many cases they do not make any deliberate verbal attempt to get you to buy the product. Unlike American commercials, Japanese commercials are not suggestive, nor do they use imperative wording. In fact, frequently one cannot even tell what is being advertised. Robert Collins (1992:130-131) describes one such Japanese commercial:

> *A man sits on the beach in a folding camp chair. The ocean ripples in the golden reflection of a setting sun. A dog at his side, the man sips reflectively from a glass of amber liquid---his head slightly bobbing, apparently in time with the music playing on his headset. The music of Bach fills the soundtrack. He crosses one denim-clad leg over the other, raises his glass, and offers a silent toast to the camera. The camera pans back, and seagulls swoop and soar over the man's head. A voice announces the name of the product.*

This is not a commercial for beer or designer jeans, but rather an ad for stomach medicine. Obviously the message is very subtle. The man wouldn't be having such a wonderful time if he were at home with intestinal distress. Collins goes on to say that "the thrust of Japanese advertising is intended to create in the prospective customer a feeling of goodwill, confidence, and trust in the company and product without going into the details of the product's specific use or application."

Simply put, in certain Asian societies rhetorical ambiguity is so common that successful communication depends on a sensitivity to the nonverbal context. Other speech communities, such as certain Arabic cultures, are equally imprecise, but for exactly the opposite reason. That is, they engage in over-assertion, exaggeration, and repetition. The Arabic language is filled with forms of verbal exaggeration. For example, certain common ending words are meant to be emphasized; frequently certain pronouns will be repeated in order to fully dramatize the message; highly graphic metaphors and similes are common; and it is not at all unusual to hear an Arabic speaker use a long list of adjectives to modify a single noun for the sake of emphasizing the point. What would be an assertive statement to a North American might appear to be weak and equivocating to an Arab. It should be kept in mind that this rhetorical feature of linguistic over-assertion is just another form of verbal inexactness because it fails to send direct, precise messages.

How These Values Play Out in Different Cultures:

Direct Cultures:

- People like to "speak their mind."
- Honesty is more highly valued than politeness.
- Communication tends to be confrontational and highly competitive.
- People are less concerned about offending the other person and causing a conflict.

- People are not particularly good at understanding nonverbal cues.
- People are seen as overly talkative, redundant, and belaboring the obvious.
- People become flustered in the absence of words. Abhorring a silence, they will fill the silence with talk, even if it is not in their own best interest.
- Employees are rewarded for their speaking skills, not their listening skills.

Indirect Cultures:

- Speech is much more guarded so as to avoid embarrassing others.
- Politeness is much more highly valued than honesty.
- Communication is nonconfrontive, supportive, and aimed at group cohesion.
- Facts will be distorted in order not to cause others to "lose face."
- People are adept at interpreting nonverbal cues.
- People are seen as non-disclosing, secretive, mysterious and untrustworthy.
- May want to use go-betweens in the conduct of business.
- Employees are rewarded for their skills of listening, not speaking.

Implications for Business: (When Dealing with Indirect Communicators)

1. Become more low-key, polite, and nonconfrontive.

2. Take a course in "active listening."

3. Help others "save face" by giving them an avenue of retreat.

4. Never take "yes" for an answer. Make sure the "yes" is not a disguised way of saying "no." Become familiar with the various indirect ways of saying "no."

5. Learn to become more comfortable with silences. Don't rush in with more words just to fill the silence.

6. Practice developing your nonverbal competence by watching your favorite television drama or sitcom with the sound turned off.

7. Lower your decibel level when talking.

8. Understand that when dealing with employees who are indirect communicators, an objective, "tell-it-like-it-is" job appraisal may not be the best way to motivate an individual to make improvements in her/his job performance.

9. Resist the temptation to exaggerate, hype, or engage in verbal overkill.

III. STRUCTURE-FLEXIBILITY

Preston Jessup has been chosen to set up a branch office in Pusan, Korea. While some of the staff will be transferred from other offices around the world, the majority of hires are to be from Pusan. Preston is particularly interested in hiring an experienced office manager and is confident that he will be able to find the right person because the firm is prepared to pay an excellent salary with generous benefits. But after following up on six different leads of potential candidates for the position, they all turn down Preston's offer. They are very appreciative of being considered for the position, but all prefer to stay with their current employers. How can you explain this unanticipated situation?

This dimension asks the question: "To what extent are people threatened by ambiguity and change?" While the unpredictability about the future is part of the human experience, cultures differ in the degree to which they tolerate ambiguity, cope with uncertainties, and adapt to the future. Over the last three decades this dimension has been referred to as "uncertainty avoidance" by Hofstede (1980), "order/flexibility" by Brake, Walker, and Walker (1995), and the "mutability" dimension by Condon and Yousef (1975). Those cultures on the "structure" end of the continuum seek to reduce uncertainty through formal rules and high levels of organizational structure. People feel uncomfortable in unstructured, ambiguous, and unpredictable situations. Such "high structure" cultures as Greece, Portugal, and Japan try to minimize unstructured situations as much as possible by (a) maintaining strict laws and regulations, (b) providing safety and security measures, (c) adhering to absolute truths, and (d) rejecting unorthodox ideas. At the other end of the continuum, people from more flexible cultures (e.g., Denmark and the United States), tend to be more tolerant of unorthodox opinions, are comfortable with fewer rules and simpler organization structures, and tend to be more relativistic in their beliefs. This structure-flexibility dimension can be depicted in the following way:

Flexible Cultures	High-Structure Cultures
Live day-by-day	Anxiety about the future
Less resistance to change	More resistance to change
More risk-taking	Less risk-taking
Will change employer	Will stay with employer
Hope for success	Fear of failure
Little loyalty to employer	Loyalty to employer
Sometimes rules can be broken	Rules not to be broken
Conflict is expected	Conflict is undesirable
Initiative encouraged	Initiative discouraged
Differences are tolerated	Differences are bad
Low stress	High stress

Little emotional expression	Expression acceptable
Superiors are fallible	Superiors are infallible
Informal organizational structures	Formal organizational structures

Now that we understand that cultures have different needs for order and structure, Preston's inability to hire local Korean employees makes more sense. When compared to people from a number of other cultures, Koreans score relatively high on Hofstede's uncertainty avoidance index. They are, in other words, uncomfortable with situations of change and are thus reluctant to rock the boat. Even if not particularly satisfied in their present jobs, they are likely to stay put because "the devil they know is better than the devil they don't know." Their present employers provide a fair amount of job security, which essentially means that they do not have to worry about the ambiguities of the future.

There is considerable variability across cultures in terms of the extent to which people feel that behavior should follow formal rules. In those societies that emphasize structure and order, behavior is rigidly prescribed, either with written laws or unwritten social codes. Even if individuals within such a society occasionally break the rules, they generally believe that it is a good thing that the rules exist. In short, people feel anxious in the absence of formal regulations. At the other polarity, more flexible societies also have rules and regulations, but they are considered more of a convenience than an absolute moral imperative. People in such societies are able to live comfortably without strict conformity to social rules, and in fact, often appreciate their freedom to "do their own thing." In terms of engaging in negotiations, people from "high-structured" societies are not very good negotiators because the outcomes of negotiations are never predictable. People from more flexible societies, on the other hand, are much more comfortable in negotiating situations in which the outcome is not a foregone conclusion.

Research conducted by Scott Shane (1995) has strongly suggested a relationship between flexible cultures and innovation. Working with a sample of over 4400 individuals from 68 different countries, Shane found that people from flexible societies are more likely to encourage innovation among their employees than are people from uncertainty avoiding societies. More specifically, Shane found that the more flexible the society, the more likely people were to (a) defend innovators against the inherently conservative organizational hierarchy, (b) persuade others to support innovation, (c) provide innovators with opportunities to violate organizational rules, and (d) provide innovators with the freedom needed to be creative. In an earlier study, Shane (1993) found that uncertainty accepting societies are more innovative than uncertainty avoiding societies. These two studies provide empirical evidence to suggest that the structure-flexibility value should be considered in the strategic decision of where innovation efforts (such as R and D facilities) are physically located.

Another study, conducted by Offermann and Hellmann (1997), examined the relationship between leadership style and structure-flexibility. By examining 425 midlevel managers from 39 different countries, they found that managers from high-structure cultures maintained higher levels of control over their employees, were less approachable, and were less willing to delegate authority. Such knowledge about structure-flexibility can be useful when hiring or promoting managers in cross-cultural situations.

Working with people from societies with different levels of uncertainty avoidance has a number of important implications for global business. For example, employees from societies with high-structure needs are likely to be resistant to both personal and organizational change because the ensuing results are unknowable ahead of time. Given their intolerance for bending the rules, they would feel more comfortable in a workplace with a highly structured (and consistently enforced) set of policies and guidelines governing their behavior. Since change is threatening, such employees would not be particularly good candidates for overseas assignments. In terms of retirement options, they would prefer to have their pension funds invested in a low interest-bearing account that provides slow growth but maximum security. Owing to their preference for avoiding the uncertainties of changing jobs, they would be unusually loyal employees, but would expect reciprocal loyalty from their employers. And finally, they would prefer to be managed by a strong and competent manager whose authority is above question.

When working with people from more flexible societies, a very different type of workforce emerges, and the implications for conducting business are also quite different. Employees are more willing to experiment with new techniques, jobs, and even organizational structures. They are more likely to function effectively in work teams and in meetings with loose agendas. Such workers are more likely to want their company to invest their pension fund in the stock market rather than in safer, less-risky investments. Since they are not threatened by workers from different cultures, they are more likely to work successfully in diverse, cross-cultural teams and would be good choices for expatriate assignments. Moreover, workers from the more flexible end of the continuum need less supervision, are likely to question the decisions made by their superiors, and tend to be more creative.

Implications for Business: (When Dealing with High-Structure Societies)

1. When working with people from societies with high uncertainty avoidance, try to minimize their anxieties about the future. In other words, build into your proposals and decisions as much predictability about the future as possible.

2. Anticipate and reward your employees for their loyalty to the organization.

3. Make modest proposals for change, not radical ones.

4. Avoid appointing managers who are younger than most of their employees.

5. To help overcome the inherent fear of failure, provide structured work experiences for your employees that are likely to produce successful outcomes.

6. Make certain that organizational guidelines (rules and regulations) are in place, explicitly stated, and adhered to.

7. Avoid being too unorthodox in your opinions and recommendations.

8. Expect that people from high uncertainty-avoidance societies will be highly rigid during negotiations. Whatever proposal you put on the negotiating table should contain built-in protections that will make the future somewhat more predictable.

9. Keep realistic expectations about your employees' personal initiative, creativity, or willingness to work in teams.

10. Be aware of the fact that most employees are not likely to appreciate a manager who delegates too much authority.

IV. CONTROL-CONSTRAINT

While teaching elementary school in rural India, Jennifer Rogers was struck by the widespread poverty of the local populations. After several months, she became disturbed that the other teachers at the school seemed to be very passive and unconcerned as to whether their students learned anything at all. Jennifer tried to convince her colleagues that these children could only rise out of poverty if they received a good education. She encouraged them to use new teaching techniques and spend more time drilling them on their lessons. But the local teachers responded by saying that they preferred to use the teaching techniques that had always been used. "And besides," they argued, "improvements in their education would not improve their destiny." Why does this response seem so strange (and irresponsible) to Jennifer?

This very important value dimension looks at how people from different cultures view the world around them. Some cultures embody the value that people should be in control of themselves and their environments. These societies are "*inner-directed*" because individuals are encouraged to impose their will upon the environment. Other cultures teach the contrasting value that control resides not with people but with external forces such as governments, fate, or the gods. These societies tend to be more "*other-directed.*" An intermediary position (represented by traditional Native

American cultures) would be that people live in harmony with their environment, neither controlling it, nor being controlled by it.

In American culture, people are encouraged to control their own lives as well as their environments. Harnessing the power of rivers, taming the wilderness, and conquering outer space are viewed as both possible and desirable. Problems, most of which are solvable, are seen as nothing more than the result of poor planning or lack of effort, not the result of some external, uncontrollable force. In such societies, humans not only can, but should, take control of their own lives and the natural world, and if need be, change it to fit their own needs. At the other extreme are those societies that view humans as being constrained by forces beyond their control (such as fate, luck, powerful governments, or supernatural forces). In rural areas of India, South American, and the Middle East, people are expected to accept things as they are, or at least not be so presumptuous as to think that they can change conditions in their lives. This value dimension looks like this:

Control	Constraint
Humans control nature	Nature controls humans
Change environment to fit human needs	Fatalism
Inner-directed	Other-directed

Jennifer's frustration can be understood more fully by first appreciating the very different views in U.S. culture and rural Indian culture concerning "locus of control." In the United States, it is believed that ultimately people are responsible for their own destiny. If a situation is not good, it is often possible for the individual to actually do something to change it. Americans, in other words, see themselves as being masters of their own lives. In India, on the other hand, and indeed throughout many other parts of the world, people have a more fatalistic outlook. Indians often feel that their lives are guided by external forces beyond their control. Thus, whether their destiny is to be rich or poor, successful or unemployed, or healthy or sick, it is predestined and cannot be changed. Since there is not anything they can do about these aspects of their lives, they simply accept them. Although this fatalism gives rural Indians courage in bad times, it also discourages efforts to change.

Since earliest times, Americans have assumed that nature and the physical environment not only can be, but should be, controlled for their own convenience. Although the early European colonialists were lured to North America with promises of a rich and abundant land, they soon discovered that the New World was a harsh, and often unforgiving, wilderness. To survive in such a wild environment required a good deal of stamina, creativity, and hard work. Since the land was so vast, early land use strategies were adopted that produced the quickest and most efficient results rather than being kind and gentle to the environment. In fact, the very harshness of the natural environment led the early settlers to believe that their survival would only be possible if this wilderness was conquered, subdued, and even transformed so as to best serve them. In many respects, the early American settlers viewed their surroundings as the "enemy," which was to be dealt with in a military fashion.

By and large, this dismal view of the natural environment---which separates humans from nature---continues into the present. Although, as we enter the new millenium, there is an upswing in environmental consciousness, the assumption that still predominates in the United States is that the natural environment should be controlled so as to serve people. If a river overflows its banks and destroys homes and crops, Americans are likely to dam it up, change its course, and dictate when, and at what speed, the water will flow out. If gravity is a barrier to walking on the moon, the American solution is to build a sufficiently large engine to propel astronauts past the earth's gravitational pull. If a mountain stands in the way of convenient travel between two points, Americans will build a super highway by slicing off the top of the mountain or tunneling through it. To most North Americans, the expression "to move a mountain" is not a metaphor symbolizing the impossible, but rather an optimistic challenge based on past experience. Moreover, we control human conception (through pills, mechanical devices, and surgical procedures) to suit our own personal timetables; and if we are having difficulty conceiving, we will intervene with fertility drugs or invitro-fertilization so that *we* control conception rather than leaving it to God, fate, or "mother nature." In short, Americans believe that given enough time, effort, and money, there is no aspect of nature that cannot be subjugated eventually to the human will.

This obsession with controlling nature leads naturally from Americans' mechanistic view of the world. The world, in other words, is a machine which humans can tinker with, adjust, rebuild if necessary, and make increasingly more efficient for the benefit of its human masters. In the short run, Americans have been reasonably successful at subjugating and transforming their mechanistic world so that it runs faster, more smoothly, and more efficiently. Over the course of the last five hundred years, Americans have altered the landscape by damming up rivers, cutting down forests, making fertile land with the help of chemical technology, reclaiming deserts, and building housing developments, cities, and shopping malls. Motivated by profits and the desire to improve the quality of life, the land has often been divided, cleared, sold, rearranged, paved over, and generally denuded of its natural wealth. While each of these man-made transformations has looked like progress, some feel that the cumulative effect has proven to be detrimental in the long run.

This mechanistic view---in which the world is subjugated to the human will---carries with it a supreme faith in quantification. If humans are to tinker with, and ultimately control, the workings of the universe, then they will need to have very accurate empirical data on everything. So, Americans have an on-going love affair with numbering, counting, and the accumulation of statistics. Americans assume that if it can be measured, then it can be controlled. Thus, they have divided their observable world into miles, acres, watts, minutes, pounds, inches, horsepower, degrees Fahrenheit, gallons, square feet, megabytes, batting averages, and nanoseconds to mention but a few measures. Even our physical space is divided into neat (usually rectangular) plots, described precisely with numbers and letters, thus enabling us to locate them easily. It is not an exaggeration to claim that American society would come to a virtual standstill if we lost our numbers (which, of course, is what made the Y2K computer problem so scary). How could we determine who gets into Princeton if we lost our SAT measurements? On what basis would we buy an automobile if we couldn't compare such features as horsepower, gas mileage, or estimated repair costs? How could airline pilots be expected to land their planes safely if they had no idea of their altitude, air speed, or fuel levels? To be certain, Americans sometimes delude themselves into thinking that they will understand (and thus gain control over) anything that they can describe in quantitative terms. On the other hand, over the last several hundred years, Americans, for good or ill, have managed to manipulate their physical environment to a greater degree than any other society in history.

Part of this American reverence for controlling nature is the desire for growth and bigness. If humans can exert their will to control nature, then as things get better, they also get bigger. The decade of the 1990s certainly has witnessed this phenomenon in the global marketplace with company mergers that have resulted in enormous corporations that control tens of billions of dollars worth of assets. Most American universities seem to be consumed with the notion of continually expanding their enrollments, and in fact, measure their worth as an institution by enrollment growth. Even our urban skylines often reflect the notion that "bigger is better." In a number of American cities, major corporations compete with one another for bragging rights to the tallest building in town, even though building such edifices might not be based on the soundest financial rationale. Thus, Americans place a high value on the bigness of something. That is, we are constantly striving for a larger quantity of assets if we run a corporation, channels if we watch cable TV, students if we run a university, bathrooms if we own a home, decibels if we lead a rock band, home runs if we play baseball, floors if we own a skyscraper, or megatons if we drive an SUV.

At the opposite end of the spectrum from the United States are those cultures that can best be described as "nature over people." In the rural, more traditional, areas of India, Sub-Saharan Africa, or Pakistan, people see themselves being dominated by, or at the mercy of, nature. This highly fatalistic position sees nature as exerting potentially harmful powers over people. To try to understand or counteract these harmful powers would be hopeless. Of course, contemporary values in these "nature-over-people" cultures are often reinforced by past experiences. If, for example, people have heard tales about how generations of their own ancestors have been at the mercy of forces beyond their control, then there is little hope or expectation that they will take control of their world.

Moreover, in many parts of the developing world the problems are so pervasive that the everyday person on the street feels overwhelmed. To illustrate, much of Sub-Saharan Africa faces staggering problems of extreme poverty, political instability, massive foreign debt, famine, warfare, illiteracy, and most recently the scourge of AIDS. The disparities in wealth and resources between most African countries and countries like the United States are staggering. For example, whereas the per capita GNP in the United States is over $27,000, it is $274 in Kenya, $134 in

Tanzania, and $96 in Ethiopia. When most Africans must face such insurmountable problems with so few of the world's resources, it is not likely that they will develop a control orientation in the foreseeable future.

It is important to realize that there is an intermediate position between the "people-over-nature" view held by Americans and the "nature-over-people" notion found in places like rural India. Some cultures of the world try to strike a proper balance between people, on the one hand, and the natural environment on the other. For example, Japanese culture emphasizes the integration of people with the natural world, whereby the natural environment shapes people and, in turn, is shaped by people.

The human-nature relationship most commonly found in the world would be some combination of those found in Japan and India. To many people, the natural world is closely associated with supernatural forces. Although natural phenomena are not necessarily envisioned in malevolent terms, the world of nature is seen as a manifestation of God, and as such, should not be influenced, much less transformed, by the human hand.

In an appreciable number of cultures outside of the United States, God is closely associated with the natural world. The sky, or heaven, for example, is thought to be where God lives and reigns. Among some cultures, mountains are seen as physical evidence of God's presence. Many people believe that certain mountains are the dwelling place of God, and it is for this reason that they face these mountains when offering their prayers. Given this worldview, it is little wonder that many non-Americans do not share our cultural desire to transform the natural environment for their own purposes. For them, the world of nature is to be respected and revered. If, in fact, such natural phenomena as rain, rivers, and mountains are conceived of as God's creations and symbols of God's presence, it would be grossly presumptuous--indeed blasphemous--for people to want to alter, control, or dominate nature. Rather, people are expected to establish the proper relationship with God, which, among other things, involves respecting and living in harmony with the world of nature.

How, then, do these two different approaches to the environment play out within a business context? In terms of marketing, we can view the totality of world markets as a natural environment with which we interact. If we are from a "control" or inner-directed society such as the United States, we are likely to view world markets as something to be conquered or dominated. By devising the proper marketing strategy (and expending a great deal of money and energy), we are likely to win over a sizeable share of the market by coercing, cajoling, or otherwise convincing people to buy our products. At the other end of the continuum, business organizations from so-called "constraint" or other-directed societies are more likely *to be shaped* by markets rather than conquering or dominating them. Whereas control societies try to have their products succeed in world markets because of sheer will, "constraint" societies are more likely to take direction from their customers. Rather than trying to force their products (that work well for them) on others, more constraint-oriented societies are likely to redesign their products to meet the needs of their customers. These organizations are, in other words, allowing the market environment to control them, at least to the extent that they are producing a new line of products more in line with customer preferences. It should come as no surprise, therefore, that some constraint societies are highly successful economic performers because they are adapting themselves to the environment.

Just as the control-constraint value dimension has implications for marketing, it also has a powerful influence in the world of management. Sales incentives, bonuses, and commissions are used widely to motivate sales personnel in control societies such as the United States. The assumption is that individual sales people, who have power to change and influence the market environment through personal effort, will be motivated by cash incentives for increasing their product sales. Yet, people from other-directed societies are likely to respond negatively to pay-for-performance sales strategies. They believe that their economic environment experiences both good times and bad times. Holding out personal incentives is meaningless because individuals are not able to change these powerful, and inevitable, trends. During hard economic times it is unfair to put undue pressure on the sales force to sell products to local people who can ill afford them. Instead, one must accept the hard times as inevitable, ride them out together, and wait patiently for economic conditions to improve. This typically "other-directed" approach stems from their view of themselves as being controlled by the external forces of their economic environment.

Implications for Business (When Dealing with "Other-directed" People):

1. Do not discount or ignore perceived constraints.

2. Be aware that you may be perceived as being immodest and overly controlling.

3. Be aware that setting unrealistically high expectations may make you come across as being naïve.

4. Facilitate change, don't force change.

5. When facilitating change, be patient and appreciate the need for consensus.

6. Realize that people may have an unrealistic view of you as someone who can accomplish anything and everything.

V. COMPETITION-COOPERATION

While teaching business English to Samoan employees, you decide to help your students learn to spell by having a "spelling bee." You divide the class into two equal teams and have them stand on opposite sides of the room. After several minutes you realize that the students are not participating with much enthusiasm nor are they having much fun. You conclude that the students are not particularly interested in learning to spell. But, could there be another explanation for the lack of enthusiasm?

All cultures must decide whether they prefer social relationships that are competitive or cooperative. Competitive societies, such as Great Britain, the United States, Germany, and Australia, tend to place a high value on winning, getting ahead, individual achievement, and personal success. Competitive societies measure success narrowly, often in terms of material gains. In addition, these societies tend to measure precisely and compare peoples' achievements in most areas of their lives. Competitive cultures encourage and reward individual achievement and train people to be aggressive, independent, and highly motivated. You are likely to hear in competitive societies such expressions as "We're number one!," "Let's get out there and win this one for the Old Gipper," or, more colloquially, "Let's kick butt."

At the other end of the continuum are cooperative societies, such as Sweden, Norway, and Denmark. In such societies, a high value is placed on empathy, nurturing, interdependence, and maintaining long-term social relation-ships. Quality of life is more important than winning or being "Number One." Whereas decisions in competitive societies are often made by individuals, in cooperative societies decision-making tends to be more consensual. In a work environment, employees are hired not primarily for their productivity, but rather for their ability to facilitate communication, demonstrate loyalty, promote shared values, and contribute to the overall work environment. In cooperative societies, you are more likely to hear such expressions as "We're all in this together" or "How can we have a win-win situation?" This competitive-cooperative dimension looks something like this:

Competitive	Cooperative
Achievement	Relationships
Being number one	Contribute to group
Individual decision-making	Consensus
Win-lose	Win-win
Aggressive	Sympathetic

If we return to the scenario above, it should become clear that your interpretation of the Samoan spelling bee was probably inaccurate. In the United States, children are encouraged in most areas of their lives to be competitive. In fact, pitting one student against another, as in a spelling bee, is a widely used technique in American schools to motivate children to learn. To win, even though others will lose, is a desirable motivational classroom strategy. But such educational techniques are not universally exportable, particularly to those societies that place a much higher value on consensus, relationship building, and cooperation. The Samoan workers, whose culture is more cooperative than competitive, reacted negatively to being thrown into the high competition of a spelling bee, a situation that no doubt appears to be selfish and mean-spirited. A more appropriate teaching technique for the Samoan classroom would have been the use of small, information-sharing groups, whereby students could have drawn on their cultural values of cooperation to teach one another how to spell.

Clearly, the operative value in the United States is competition. Most North Americans, particularly men, share with one another a strong desire to experience the "thrill of victory," while avoiding the "agony of defeat." They want to distinguish themselves at what they do, be it in their work or the games they play. From a very early age we teach our children the qualities of a winner and encourage them to emulate those qualities. Our language is replete with proverbs extolling the benefits of winning through competition:

- Competition increases desire.
- Competition is the life of trade.
- Competition makes a horse race.
- Competition is the spice of life.
- Or as former Green Bay Packer coach, Vince Lombardi, put it, "Winning isn't everything; it's the only thing."

To be winners, people in the United States must compete, and there are many opportunities to hone those competitive skills from a very early age. As pre-schoolers, boys in the United States play cops and robbers, cowboys and Indians, and "King of the Mountain." This latter game is a very appropriate metaphor for American society, for it teaches young boys to emphasize achievement, success, and competitiveness. The winner of this game is the one who literally can scramble to the top of the mountain and hold it against all the other boys in the game. It gives the winner, however briefly, a sense of what it feels like to be the best, the sole victor against the entire field of competitors.

By the time they get to school, children compete for grades, class-standing, and on standardized examinations such as the SATs so they can compete to get into a good college. Competition is as much a part of the extracurricular activities of school life as it is of the academic component. Students are encouraged to compete for election to student government offices and on projects in such organizations as scouting, 4-H, and Junior Achievement. In recent years, youth have taken to playing computer games with a competitive focus. And, of course, they are expected to compete on the athletic fields. Children who might enjoy running or throwing a ball just for the fun of it are usually put on a team, given a uniform, and encouraged to be "number one." Whether academic or extra-curricular, young people grow up in an environment where competition is encouraged, considered virtuous, and rewarded.

While most Americans are reluctant to admit it, our high value on competition leads us to the inescapable conclusion that much of the success we achieve is gained at the expense of others. Nowhere is this more obvious than in the system of "grading on the curve" used in many American schools. By grading all students in a class *relative to one another*, the teacher is relegating those at the bottom to failure, quite apart from how well they might perform. In some highly competitive environments, students may even subvert their classmates by stealing reserved readings or tearing pages out of library books. This turns some classrooms into "armed camps," whereby students are afraid to engage in cooperative learning with their classmates because they fear that if they help a classmate learn the material, they themselves will be left behind.

Our laissez-faire economic system is based on the principle of competition. That is, it is assumed that prices will be kept low while the quality of goods and services will remain high as long as competition exists. To prevent the constraint of competition in the U.S. marketplace, the U.S. Department of Justice, through its Anti-Trust Division, is empowered to act as a watchdog against the development of monopolies. It is, in fact, this strong U.S. value of competition that has led to the recent lawsuit brought by the Justice Department against Microsoft for constraint of trade.

The legal system in the United States, based on an adversarial process, relies on competition for the administration of justice. Such a system is predicated on the assumption that justice will be served when plaintiff and defendant *compete* with one another to marshal the most and best legal arguments, facts, and precedents. The United States, a highly competitive society, has 16 times as many lawyers per person than are found in Japan, a highly cooperative society (Moran, Harris, and Stripp, 1993:94).

Even adult recreation in the United States, to a large extent, tends to be based on competition. As spectators, we follow our favorite players and teams as they compete for the best batting averages, field goal percentages, or win-loss records. Much of our own leisure time is devoted to playing games (which, of course, have winners and losers) such as bridge, golf, tennis, or Trivial Pursuit. It is not a coincidence that the most popular table board game of all time in the United States is Monopoly. People of all ages have played this game for the past four generations. Monopoly is so popular because it is a microcosm of American society. It allows us to play a game that simulates life. Our capitalistic economy encourages (and rewards) the individual for accumulating as much wealth as possible. If we extend that economic philosophy to its logical conclusion, it would be possible for a single individual, through hard work and unfettered competition, to accumulate so much of a particular item that he or she would achieve a monopoly. But the game of Monopoly allows us to play at what is virtually impossible to achieve in life---i.e., a monopoly on everything. The winner of the game of Monopoly gets absolutely everything (property, utilities, railroads, and cash) for him/herself, while wiping everyone else off the board! The winner gets it all, while the losers get nothing. Each time an American plays the game of Monopoly, it reinforces the notion of competition, achievement, and winning.

The value placed on competition in the United States is certainly evident in our linguistic style. Typically, verbal communication, particularly among men, is used for self-assertion, highlighting one's ideas, and establishing one's status and power. Discourse is often adversarial and argumentative, with the desired outcome being winning others over to our own point of view. If we look at course offerings from speech and communications departments at American universities, we find such titles as "Argumentation and Debate," "Advanced Persuasion," and "Public Advocacy." Discourse in the United States often deals directly with controversial issues, is sometimes emotional, and has been described as "in your face." Sometimes we even preface our words with the phrase, "Just for the sake of argument."

Linguist Deborah Tannen (1998) has suggested that the adversarial nature of communication in the United States has escalated so sharply in recent years that we have become an "argument culture." According to Tannen, public discourse---in our media, politics, courtrooms, and classrooms---is becoming increasingly warlike. This makes us approach most subjects as a conflict between two opposing sides. The way we now explore the news is to set up a "debate" between representatives from the two most extremely polarized positions and let them slug it out. It is this highly-charged, ultra-competitive mindset that brings us such "public affairs" programming as "Crossfire," "Hardball," and "Equal Time." American politics has become so contentious in the last decade that a record number of fourteen Senators in 1996 chose not to stand for re-election because of the escalating rancor and partisanship. Even the normally mild-mannered academics today cannot seem to write a scholarly article without debunking someone else's position. Tannen's thesis is that public dialogue in the United States has become increasingly combative, to the extent that we now tend to approach any philosophical or policy issue as a fight.

While some level of competition is universal, there are some cultures that tend to emphasize cooperation rather than competition. Even in their games, the final goal is not to produce a winner and a loser. Some societies play games that involve camaraderie and group effort, such as all participants trying to keep a ball in the air without it hitting the ground. Among certain small scale, closely knit societies, such as the Inuit or the Hopi, competition that could lead to conflict was viewed as socially disruptive. While the Hopi Indians were fond of foot races, it was considered socially inappropriate to outdistance or "show up" the other runners. The goal was to finish together, not to have a winner and a bunch of losers.

This same lack of competitiveness---in stark contrast to what might be anticipated in the United States---was related by Otto Klineberg in his description of how performance on IQ tests varied cross-culturally because some cultures stressed cooperation and group problem-solving rather than competition. Klineberg (1969:66) relates the experience of a social scientist administering an IQ test to a group of Australian aborigines. Although each subject was expected to solve each task individually, it proved to be a most uncomfortable situation for the test-takers, who were accustomed to solving problems in groups by means of a consensus process. The subjects could not understand why the examiner, whom they considered their friend, would not help them solve the problems. The aborigines, accustomed as they were to group deliberation and problem-solving, remained perplexed throughout the examination, as they would continually pause for approval and assistance from the examiner. Not surprisingly, the test scores were not high because of this near total absence of cultural familiarity with the competitive mode.

When we move away from small-scale societies such as the Hopi or the Australian aborigines, we can see how direct competition on an everyday basis is also avoided in such large-scale societies as China and Japan. To be certain, competition exists in these countries, both in business and society, but it is expressed much less directly. Workers are not singled out for personal recognition, but rather *group* accomplishments and accountability are emphasized. Harmony is the order of the day, while confrontations and conflicts are studiously avoided. Verbal communication is much less competitive, emphasizing instead compromise and conciliation. Whereas communication in the United States is "in your face," the Japanese and Chinese are more interested in "saving face" by avoiding confrontation. Americans sometimes use their emotions to further emphasize the righteousness of their position. People from cooperative societies, on the other hand, suppress their emotions in an attempt to be polite (which usually causes Americans to think of the Japanese as sly, secretive, and inscrutable). And, by concentrating more on listening (and observing the nonverbal cues), Japanese communicators, while still desiring a favorable outcome, are less willing to bludgeon the other person with a barrage of powerful words for the sake of winning through verbal intimidation.

Implications for Business (When Dealing with Cooperative Societies)

1. Rather than pitting one manager or salesperson against another, focus on group responsibility and group honor.

2. Learn to be an active listener, rather than trying to win an argument.

3. Blame should be communicated indirectly, not directly.

4. Avoid calling attention to a member of the workforce, either positively or negatively, particularly in front of others.

5. In marketing, managing, or negotiating, avoid self-promotion and obvious attempts to win people over.

6. Look for win-win solutions to problems.

7. Don't mistake politeness for the absence of either competitiveness or the desire to win.

8. You should be competitive, but refrain from being boastful or projecting a winner-takes-all position.

9. Avoid making threats.

Cross-cultural Quiz (Answers on pages 202-203)

1. While on a business trip to Canberra, Australia, you need to take a taxi from one business meeting to another. You signal to a taxi on the street by waving your right hand, jump into the back seat, and tell the driver where you want to go. As he starts to pull away, however, the driver turns to you and says: "What's wrong, Mate? Do you think I have leprosy?" What does he mean by this?

2. Renee Griffith was sent by her accounting firm to Kuala Lumpur, Malaysia for a month-long assignment. During her first week in the office she was introduced to the nine-year old daughter of one of her Malaysian colleagues who had stopped by the office with her mother. Renee was so taken by the young girl's beauty that she patted her on the head and told her parents what a gorgeous daughter they had. Much to Renee's surprise, however, the girl's mother responded by saying that she really wasn't very attractive and then abruptly left with the girl. What had Renee done to cause the mother to react in such a way?

3. Ralph Ackerman, a senior executive working for several years in his company's office in Brussels, wanted to make a good impression on his Belgium staff. His predecessor had

told him that it would be particularly difficult for him, or any American, to get to know his subordinates.   In order to facilitate good relations with his staff, Ralph decided to do several things.   First, he arrived at the office early in the morning so he could visit with his subordinates over coffee. Second, he initiated an "open-door" policy so that everyone would feel free to stop by and chat. However, in spite of his best efforts, Ralph ended up alienating his subordinates. What could Ralph have done differently in this situation?

CHAPTER 5

VERBAL COMMUNICATION

The world of global business, like any global environment, requires effective communication in order to operate efficiently. Global players need to be effective communicators at a number of levels. One must communicate with employees, customers, suppliers, and host government officials. Effective communication among people from the same culture is often difficult enough. But when attempting to communicate with people who do not speak your language---and who have different ideas, attitudes, assumptions, perceptions, and ways of doing things---one's chances for miscommunication increase enormously.

People communicate in two ways. The most obvious communication mode is language, the use of words that have mutually understood meanings and are linked together into sentences according to consistently followed rules. A less obvious, and more frequently overlooked, form of communication is nonverbal communication, or what Edward T. Hall (1959) refers to as the "silent language." The next two chapters examine the nature of communication in international business and how communication problems can develop when people communicate, or attempt to communicate, across cultures. This chapter will focus on language, while the next will look at the nonverbal aspects of communication.

WHAT IS LANGUAGE?

The term language, like so many others that we think we understand, is far more complex than we might imagine. Language, which is found in all cultures of the world, is a symbolic system of sounds that, when put together according to a certain set of rules, conveys meanings to its speakers. The meanings attached to any given word in all languages are totally *arbitrary*. That is, the word cow has no particular connection to the large bovine animal that the English language refers to as a cow. The word cow is a no more or less reasonable word for that animal than would be kaflumpha, sporge, or four-pronged squirter. The word cow does not look like a cow, sound like a cow, or have any particular physical connection to a cow. The only explanation for the use of the word is that somewhere during the evolution of the English language the word cow came to be used to refer to a large domesticated animal that gives an abundant quantity of milk. Other languages use totally different, and equally arbitrary, words to describe the very same animal.

Given the very arbitrary nature of languages, it should come as no surprise that there is enormous linguistic diversity among human populations. Even though linguists do not agree on precisely how many discrete languages exist, a reasonable estimate would be 6,000. The criterion used to establish such estimates is *mutual unintelligibility*. That is, linguists assume that if people can understand one another, they speak the same language; if they are unable to understand one another, they speak different languages.

THE NEED FOR LINGUISTIC COMPETENCE

It is the premise of this book that if global businesspeople are to be successful, they will need an intimate acquaintance with both the language and the culture of those with whom they are conducting business. Even though this seems like an eminently reasonable proposition, it is surprising to realize how many American businesspeople are totally monolingual. Of course, this is not a situation that is unique to business people. It is, rather, a national problem. The United States remains the only country in the world where it is possible to earn a university degree without speaking a second language. Not only can it be done, but in actual fact, most university graduates in the United States never do master a second language. As we enter the 21st century, there are over 10,000 Americans attempting to do business in Japan, and fewer than 5 percent speak any Japanese whatsoever. And, then, we have the unmitigated gall to wonder why those "sneaky Japanese" don't want to buy our products. How would we feel if the shoe were on the other foot? If a Japanese vacuum cleaner salesman came to our house trying to sell us the world's best vacuum cleaner, but he couldn't speak a lick of English, would we buy his vacuum cleaner? Probably not! We can no longer afford to conduct our global affairs according to the brilliant advice: "If English was good enough for Jesus Christ, it's good enough for me."

One of the explanations offered for not learning to speak another language is because English is rapidly becoming the international language of business. Americans became spoiled during much of the 20th century. We simply assumed that since our products were so highly desired, the rest of the world would come to us to buy, and they would speak our language to boot. But, the world has become radically more competitive during the late 20th and early 21st centuries. Nigerians are now making high-quality steel while the Swedes are manufacturing and marketing world-class chain saws throughout the world. And, literally anyone can become a marketer today with the advent of the Internet. Thus, English is now just one of the major languages of the global marketplace and the mother tongue of only 5 percent of the world's population. So, if we are to be successful in the global marketplace, we must realize that the customers' language---wherever it is spoken---has a distinct sales value.

This is particularly true in those cultures that insist on building personal relationships as a prerequisite for doing business. The western salesperson who can converse, schmooze, and speak intelligently about local affairs *in the local language*, will likely gain both the business and the respect of his foreign customers.

Thus, second language proficiency increases the level of rapport with your foreign business counterparts. This in itself should be ample justification for speaking a second language. But, another very compelling reason for second language competence is that it provides a window on the "worldview" of another culture. When you learn another language, you are actually learning how the speakers of that language categorize and sort the world around them. That is, their language sets their basic mental categories, which enable them to group certain things together while keeping other things distinct. By understanding the mental categories of the speakers of another language, you are really able to see how they perceive the world, which will, no doubt, be different from the way you perceive the world.

Yet, even when you take second language learning seriously, there are many hazards along the way. Because one language never translates exactly into another language, opportunities to miscommunicate across languages are ever-present. The international business literature is filled with examples of linguistic miscues when attempting to translate advertising slogans abroad. For example, Frank Purdue of the Purdue Chicken Company decided to translate his successful U.S. slogan into Spanish as part of a major South American marketing campaign. The only way that the slogan "It takes a tough man to make a tender chicken" could be translated into Spanish was "It takes a virile man to make a chicken affectionate." More recently, the highly successful ad campaign of the American Dairy Association ("Got milk?") was translated into Spanish as "Are you lactating?" In other instances of imprecise translations, U.S. firms have advertised cigarettes with low "asphalt" (instead of tar), computer "underwear" (instead of software), and "wet sheep" (instead of hydraulic rams). As amusing as these examples may seem, such translation errors have cost U.S. firms millions of dollars in losses over the years, not to mention the damage done to their credibility and reputations.

It is important to keep in mind that U.S. firms do not have a monopoly on linguistic *faux pas*. Even when people think they know English, they frequently convey messages they don't particularly intend to send. Consider these linguistic examples of what the airline industry refers to as "near misses."

- A sign in a Romanian hotel informing the English-speaking guests that the elevator was not working read, "The lift is being fixed. For the next few days we regret that you will be unbearable" (Besner, 1982:53).
- A laundry in Rome suggests, "Ladies, leave your clothes here and spend the afternoon having a good time" (Bello, 1987).
- Reporting to his firm's headquarters, an African representative of an electronics firm referred to the "throat-cutting competition" when in fact he meant "cut-throat competition" (Salmans, 1979:46).

In all these examples, it is clear that the translators knew the language, but not well enough. Even though they knew most of the words and how to put them together, they still managed to send unintended messages.

When traveling to other English speaking countries, we are not immune from linguistic gaffes. The differences between British English and American English can be stunning. When Americans travel to the U.K., a whole list of new words confront them. The British don't line up, they "queue up"; they don't go to the drug store, they go to the "chemist shop"; and they don't put out their trash can, they put out their "dust bin." Even the British automobile can be confusing for the American. The Brits have a boot rather than a trunk, a bonnet rather than a hood, a hooter rather than a horn, and a windscreen rather than a windshield. Moreover, as an American, you may be in for quite a surprise when your British colleague, in a genuine attempt to pay a compliment, refers to your wife as "homely," for in the United States the word means "plain" or "ugly" but in the United Kingdom it means "warm" and "friendly."

THERE ARE NO INFERIOR LANGUAGES

Until the turn of the century, western linguists were convinced that European languages were superior to all others in terms of elegance, efficiency, and beauty. It was generally assumed that small-scale, nonwestern cultures, characterized by simple technologies, had equally simple languages. In other words, nonwestern people were thought to have primitive languages with a limited capacity for expressing abstract ideas. Today, however, linguists have abandoned the notion of inferior languages. Based on studies from all over the world, linguists have demonstrated time and again that people from technologically simple societies are no less capable of expressing abstract ideas than are people living in high-technology societies.

To illustrate this point, we can compare the English language with that of a traditionally technologically simple society: the Navajo people of the American Southwest. It is true that Navajo speakers are unable to make certain grammatical distinctions commonly made in English. For example, Navajo has no separate noun forms for singular and plural (such as are found in English with the -s in dogs or the -ren in children); the third person pronoun is both singular and plural and does not specify gender (it can be translated he, she, it, or they, depending on the context); and there are no adjectives because the role of the adjective to describe nouns in English is played by the verb in Navajo.

Although the Navajo language does not make the same grammatical distinctions as does the English language, in other areas it can express certain information with considerably more precision and efficiency than English. To illustrate, making a vague statement such as "I am going" is impossible in the Navajo language. Because of the structure of this language, the verb stem would include additional information on whether the person is going on foot, by horseback, in a wagon, by boat, or in an airplane. If the selected verb form indicates that the person is going on horseback, it is necessary to further differentiate by verb form whether the horse is walking, trotting, galloping, or running. Thus, in the Navajo language a great deal of information is conveyed in the single verb form that is selected to express the concept of going. To be certain, the grammatical systems of the English and Navajo languages are very different. The English language can convey all of the same information, but it requires a far larger number of words. Nevertheless, it is hardly reasonable to conclude that one is more efficient at expressing abstract ideas than the other.

LANGUAGE AND CULTURE

It is widely accepted today that it would be difficult, if not impossible, to understand a culture without first understanding its language. And it would be equally impossible to understand a language outside of its cultural context. For this reason, any effective language teacher will go beyond vocabulary and grammar by teaching students something about such topics as eating habits, values, and behavior patterns of native speakers.

How does culture influence language? As a general rule, the vocabulary of any language tends to emphasize the words that are considered to be adaptively important in that culture. This notion, known as *cultural emphasis*, is reflected in the size and specialization of vocabulary. For example, in Standard American English, we find large numbers of words that refer to technological gadgetry (such as tractor, microchip, and intake valve) and occupational specialties (such as teacher, plumber, CPA, and pediatrician) for the simple reason that technology and occupation are points of cultural emphasis in our culture. Thus, the English language helps North Americans adapt effectively to their culture by providing a vocabulary well suited for that culture. Other cultures have other areas of emphasis. The Inuit people of the Arctic have large numbers of words for snow, ice, and seals, all three of which play a vital role in their adaptation to the environment and, indeed, in their survival. In addition to a general term for seal, the Inuit language contains specific words referring to a seal basking in the sun and a seal floating on a piece of ice, as well as a number of terms for seals of different age and sex.

In small-scale cultures such as the Inuit, where most people's lives revolve around hunting or herding, areas of cultural emphasis are quite obvious. In middle-class American culture, which tends to be more complex occupationally, it is not always easy to identify a single area of cultural emphasis. Nevertheless, sports is an area of life in U.S. culture that can be shared by people from a wide variety of occupational or class backgrounds. Consequently, as Hickerson (1980:118) points out, we have many colloquialisms in American English that stem from the game of baseball, our "national pastime":

- He made a grandstand play.
- She threw me a curve.
- She fielded my questions well.
- You're way off base.

- You're batting 1000 (500, zero) so far.
- What are the ground rules?
- I want to touch all the bases.
- He went to bat for me.
- He has two strikes against him.
- That's way out in left field.
- He drives me up the wall.
- She's a team player (a clutch player).
- He's an oddball (screwball).
- Its just a ballpark estimate.

But just as culture influences language, the opposite is also true. For decades linguists have been interested in how language influences culture and behavior. Some actually believe that language is more than a symbolic inventory of experience and the physical world. Rather, they would suggest that language actually *shapes our thoughts and perceptions.* In other words, it is generally thought that, to some degree, different cultures see the world differently because of their different linguistic categories. Thus, language is more than a vehicle for communication; it actually establishes mental categories that predispose people to see things in a certain way. For example, if my language has a single word---aunt---that refers to my mother's sister, my father's sister, my mother's brother's wife, and my father's brother's wife, it is likely that I will perceive all of these family members as genealogically equivalent, and consequently, will behave toward them in basically the same way.

Since the 1960s, a number of linguists have attempted to test this notion of language influencing behavior. One study concluded that the very content of what is said by bilingual people varies according to which language is being spoken. Working with bilingual Japanese-American women in San Francisco, Ervin-Tripp (1964:96) found that the responses to the same question given at different times by the same women varied significantly depending on the language used.

To illustrate, when asked in English to finish the statement "Real friends should ... ," the respondent answered, "be very frank"; when asked the same question in Japanese at a different time, she answered "help each other." Or, when asked, "When my wishes conflict with my family ... ," the response in English was "I do what I want"; but in Japanese, the response was, "It is a time of great unhappiness." In other words, when the question was asked in Japanese, the bilingual respondent was more likely to give a "typical" Japanese response, and when questioned in English, she was more likely to give a "typical" American response. This is the type of evidence that strongly suggests that language influences or channels perceptions, which, in turn, affects what people say and how they behave.

This is just one way of demonstrating how language influences culture. The implications of this idea for the well-informed global businessperson are obvious. The notion that linguistically different people not only communicate differently but also think and perceive the world differently can be very useful. By learning the local language, the globally savvy businessperson will acquire a vehicle of communication as well as a better understanding of why people think and behave as they do.

LANGUAGE REFLECTS VALUES

In addition to reflecting its worldview, a language also reveals a culture's basic values. In chapters three and four, we discussed the nature of comparative values found throughout the world. Whether a culture is individualistic or group-oriented, will be reflected in its language and linguistic style. One such indicator of how our language reflects individualism is the number of words found in any American English dictionary that are compounded with the word "self." To illustrate, one is likely to find in any standard English dictionary no fewer than 150 such words including "self-appointed," "self-centered," "self-confident," "self-conscious," "self-educated," "self-image," "self-improvement," "self-regard," and "self-supporting." This list of English terms related to the individual (most of which carry a positive connotation) is significantly larger than those found in more group-oriented cultures. In such group-oriented cultures as Japan, people strive for the good of the larger group, such as the family, the community, or the whole society. Rather than stressing the well being of the individual, the Japanese are more concerned with justice (for group members) and righteousness (of group members). In Japan, the "We" always comes before the "I," the group is always more predominant than the individual. As Condon (1984:9) reminds us, "If Descartes had been Japanese, he would have said, 'We think, therefore we are.' "

This fundamental difference in American and Japanese values is reflected in the communication styles found in the two cultures. Because the Japanese emphasize group affiliation, they try to achieve group harmony and consensus; they avoid self-praise; they are more cooperative, compromising, and conciliatory; and they don't like to interrupt or be interrupted. By way of contrast, the communication style of most Americans involves insuring the expression of individual opinions (at whatever cost it may have on others within earshot). Americans favor a competitive, more adversarial style, which aims at winning, as in a debate. In fact, Americans tend to be confrontational, even provocative, in their attempts to make a point. While Americans often use the expression "just for the sake of argument," such an expression in the Japanese language does not exist. Japanese discourse avoids controversial issues at all costs, while Americans, with their "in-your-face" style, are quick to express controversial issues. Another difference is that Americans place great emphasis on getting their message across, while Japanese emphasize patience, politeness, and the art of listening. In the U.S., we tend to be our most "enchanted listeners," because we have a tendency of turning a dialogue to ourselves. If a friend is talking about a recent trip to Disney World, Americans are likely to talk about their own previous trip to Disney World, what they liked about it, what annoyed them, and what were some of their more memorable experiences. The Japanese are likely to be more attentive to the friend telling about his or her trip.

As was also pointed out in Chapter Three, Americans tend to be highly egalitarian, while Japanese are more attentive to, and respectful of, social hierarchy. As with individual-collectivism, this value contrast is similarly reflected in the communication patterns of both cultures. Japanese discourse is formal, ritualized, and prefers the use of titles and surnames. It is very much influenced by the relative status of the two communicants. When speaking with a senior person, a Japanese would not use the second person singular (you), as in the question, "Will you leave today?" Instead, the more junior person would ask, "Will Watanabe sensei (teacher) leave today?" The senior person is expected to initiate the discussion in Japan. It is considered inappropriate to try to engage him against his will or to ask a series of questions in an attempt to engage him. In general, the senior person is shown greater respect and deference, *honorifics* (formal linguistic constructions that enable the speaker to express minute gradations of social respect) are used, and such nonverbal behavior as posture, facial expression, and bowing are used to show this deference. Americans, by way of contrast, have a general aversion to ritual and formality. They don't like to "stand on ceremony," and they like getting on a first name basis quickly.

In addition, Japanese and American language styles are greatly influenced by the value each group places on words. Americans are so much more verbal than are the Japanese. From the earliest days of infancy, an American child is surrounded by words and is encouraged to talk. Adults hang on a child's every word, and children are rewarded for being verbally agile. Our formal educational system tends to emphasize verbal self-expression through courses in public speaking and debate clubs. Most Americans have been socialized to believe that it is wrong *not* to talk when we are in a social situation. At cocktail parties, for example, we frequently pick a topic and start talking, largely for the sake of filling up air space. In short, in the United States there has been a strong emphasis on the verbal tradition.

By way of contrast, the Japanese are admired for their modesty and lack of eloquence. This contrast can be seen in the amount of verbiage found in both societies. Research (Satoshi and Klopf, 1975) suggests that the average American spends approximately seven hours per day in conversation as compared to about half that amount for the Japanese. As Japanese turn inward toward their own intimate social groups, verbal disclosure becomes less necessary. If there is close rapport between two people, they would suggest, why do they need to communicate verbally? They already know what the other is thinking. The need to use words, according to the Japanese, implies a lack of understanding.

This general distrust of words in Japan is captured in their proverbs "Words are the root of all evil" and "The pheasant that remains silent avoids the hunter." Instead, Japanese prefer to rely on body language. The extent to which Japanese rely on nonverbal, rather than verbal, communication was illustrated by Christopher (1983:44), who spoke of an American journalist friend of his who was interviewing a senior Japanese politician:

> *Toward the end of the conversation, my friend asked how many months the politician thought it would be until the then Prime Minister of Japan would be forced to resign. For his own reasons, the politician apparently wanted my friend to have the right answer to that question and to publish it. But that posed a problem: the old man clearly felt that with a foreigner, even a knowledgeable foreigner, he could not rely on haragei (body language), and yet a lifetime of habit prevented him from giving the answer straight out. In the end, what he did was*

mutter repeatedly "Muzukashii ne" ("A difficult question."), meanwhile using his forefinger to trace very conspicuously on his desktop the number 7.

LANGUAGE AND SOCIAL CONTEXT

Learning a second language, particularly for adults, is never easy. Yet even after mastering the vocabulary, grammar, and syntax of a second language, meanings can still be obscured because of the situational use of language. After learning the formal aspects of a language, you must ask yourself, "How do people actually use their language(s) differently in different social situations?" People who speak more than one language are likely to switch between languages depending on the *social situation*. For example, a Chicano teenager from Los Angeles may speak English in his high school classroom, but Spanish at home. But even those who are monolingual often speak different *forms* of the same language depending on the social situation. To illustrate, the language that a college sophomore might use with a roommate would be appreciably different from that used when talking to his grandparents; or the choice of expressions heard in a football locker room would hardly be appropriate in a job interview. In short, what is said and how it is said are often influenced by such variables as the age, sex, and relative social status of the speakers. Whether we are talking about selectively using different languages or variations of the same language, the process is known as *code switching*.

What can we tell about the social relationships between two people from the language they use with each other? The analysis of *terms of address* can be particularly useful in this regard. Professor Green, for example, could be addressed as Dr. Green, Ma'am, Professor, Ms. Green, Elizabeth, Darling, Doc, Prof, or Beth, depending on who is doing the addressing. One would not expect that her mother or husband would refer to her as Ma'am or that her students would call her Beth. Instead, we would expect that the term of address chosen would reflect appropriately the relative social status of the two parties. In middle-class American society, the reciprocal use of first names indicates a friendly, informal relationship between equals. The reciprocal use of titles followed by last names indicates a more formal relationship between equals. The non-reciprocal use of first names and titles is found among people of unequal status. We would also expect that the same person might use different terms of address for Professor Green in different social situations. Her husband might call her Beth at a cocktail party, Darling when they are making love, and Elizabeth when engaged in an argument.

There are no speech communities that are absolutely homogeneous. Variations in language usage, known as *dialects*, are found in all language groups and can be confusing when trying to communicate in another language. It is not at all uncommon for certain dialects in complex speech communities to be considered substandard or inferior to others. Such claims are made on social or political rather than linguistic grounds. As a way of keeping minorities in their place, majority populations often consider minority dialects to be inferior. People who are not from the South regard certain "Southernisms" such as "y'all" (as in the statement, "Y'all come by and see us now") as quaint or colorful regional expressions at best or inferior and inappropriate incursions into Standard American English at worst. A more obvious example would be majority attitudes toward the nonstandard English dialect used by some Black American communities. Clearly, such usages as "You be going home" or "Don't nobody go nowhere" will never appear on major network newscasts. Although such expressions are considered to be inferior by the speakers of Standard English, these forms demonstrate logically consistent grammatical patterns and in no way prevent the expression of complex or abstract ideas. Nonstandard English should not be viewed as simply a series of haphazard mistakes in Standard English. Rather it is a fully efficient language with its own unique set of grammatical rules that are consistently applied. Thus, in linguistic terms, ghetto English is no less efficient than the language of the rich and powerful.

How language is used in any society also depends on the gender of the speaker. In some societies, men and women speak different forms of the language. That is, these languages have certain pairs of words, which carry the same meaning, but men will use one word and women the other. But, in all societies, including our own, linguistic style differs between women and men. These linguistic gender differences in the United States (called *genderlects*) have been the subject of a best-selling book by Deborah Tannen (1990). Women and men in the United States, according to Tannen, have different linguistic styles and communication goals. Women engage in "rapport-talk" and men use "report-talk." Rapport-talk characteristic of women seeks to establish connections, negotiate relationships, and reach agreement. Women's speech tends to be cooperative in character in that women acknowledge one another's contributions, use more emotional self-disclosure, and engage in more active listening. Report-talk, in contrast, is a male mode of discourse that is more competitive. Men's conversations are less social, more individualistic, and aim at controlling the flow of talk. In cross-gender conversations, men tend to dominate women by talking more, interrupting women more often, and focusing the conversation on the topics of their own choice.

SOME ADDITIONAL CONFOUNDING FACTORS: SLANG, EUPHEMISMS, AND HUMOR

To function effectively in any language community, it is necessary to know not only the formal structure of the language (vocabulary and grammar, for example) but also how it is used in different social situations. To further complicate the learning of another language, most languages, for a variety of cultural reasons, employ certain nonstandard forms such as slang, euphemism, and humor.

Slang: Slang is an informal form of a language noted for its liveliness, brevity, novelty, and often, humor. While much slang found in any language is faddish and short-lived, some words are retained for long periods of time and actually may become a part of the standard language. Slang, which can be metaphorical, playful, startling, and even offensive, often pokes fun at pretentiousness. We should not think of slang as being merely lower-class street talk, for it often includes the specialized jargon of sub-cultural groups within the society, such as businesspeople, computer buffs, truck drivers, jazz musicians, and sports announcers. The reason that slang presents a problem to those learning a new language is that there is little clue as to what the slang word means. For example, Americans refer to a crazy person as nuts, bonkers, or loony; someone who is drunk is stewed, hammered, shit-faced, plastered, smashed, or looped; and those people who are not "uptight" or "wired" are laid back, mellow, or chilled out. Thus, slang is problematic because it increases the possible variations of expressions in any given speech community.

Euphemisms: In all known societies, there are certain categories of words that should be avoided in normal, polite parlance. In many, but certainly not all, cases, the prohibited words are associated with sexual relations and everyday bodily functions such as menstruating, urinating, and defecating. Whatever words may be deemed to be taboo by a language, it is a fairly arbitrary process because a word prohibited in one speech community may be perfectly acceptable in another. Taboo words are dealt with through the use of euphemisms—that is, by substituting a bland, vague, or indirect expression for one thought to be too direct, harsh, or blunt. Euphemisms are often used to make unsavory things sound much better than they are. Americans today no longer get fired, they are *outplaced* or *nonrenewed*. Corporations can conceal fundamental structural problems by *down-sizing*, *right-sizing*, or *re-engineering*. The military, of course, is notorious for its use of euphemisms. They don't retreat, but rather *tactically re-deploy* their troops; and they use the term *pre-emptive strike* to disguise the fact that they attacked first. Moreover, Americans use a host of euphemisms to make their occupations sound less dreary than they are in reality: mechanics are referred to as *automotive internists*, garbage collectors are *sanitation engineers*, and cab drivers are called *urban transportation specialists*. Again, the existence of euphemisms presents yet another obstacle to second language learning for the international businessperson. The learner must become familiar with the prevailing value system of the particular speech community in order to understand which topics can legitimately be dealt with in a direct and straightforward manner. Without such an understanding, it will be impossible to know when to use a bland expression and when not to.

Humor: Humor is another aspect of language that tends to confuse the new language learner. While it is true that there are no known cultures that lack humor, what is perceived as being funny varies enormously from one culture to another. In some cultures, like the British and North American, humor is used in business meetings and, in fact, business presentations often start with a humorous anecdote. In other cultures, however, business is considered no joking matter. It is not unusual at international business conferences, particularly in Asia, to hear the interpreter say, "The American is now telling a joke. When he finishes, the polite thing to do is to laugh." Often jokes are told in an international business context when, in fact, it is inappropriate to use humor in such situations. But, even if humor is appropriate, the meaning of the joke or humorous story is frequently lost because it doesn't translate well from one language to another.

Jokes are difficult to understand because they contain a good deal of information about the culture of the joke teller. In order to "get" the joke, the listener must understand these pieces of cultural information and how they are combined to make something funny. The long-standing joke in the United States about lawyers is a case in point. "Why do lawyers not have to worry about sharks when they vacation at the beach?" The answer: "Professional courtesy." In order to appreciate the humor, the listener would have to know several pieces of *cultural* information about the United States: (a) that sharks have been known to attack Americans while swimming, (b) that lawyers in the United States, like sharks, have the reputation of preying on people, and (c) that members of some professions in the United States give special considerations to other members of their profession. And, assuming the listener did understand these culture-specific pieces of information, he or she would still need to appreciate the idea that humor in the United States is found in ridiculing an entire profession of people. Asians, however, with their strong tradition of Buddhism and Confucianism, place a high value on politeness and face-saving for others and would find little to laugh about in this type of sarcasm or parody.

Humor tends to be so culture-specific that it is usually a good entrée into understanding the culture of the teller of the joke. Jokes, in other words, tell you a good deal about what is valued in a particular culture. To illustrate, there is a contemporary joke in the U.S. about the attractive young woman who asks the old man, "Would you like super sex?" His response, "I think I'll take the soup" reflects the generally negative stereotypes that most Americans have concerning the elderly; that is, that they have no interest in sex, are hard of hearing, or are so mentally diminished that they don't know the difference between soup and sex. While Americans like to joke about getting old, people from many parts of Asia, Africa, and South America have the highest regard for the elderly. Thus, such an attempt at humor would not only be not funny, it would be offensive.

CONCLUSION

It should be apparent by now that becoming fluent in another language is no easy matter, particularly if you are trying to master that second language as an adult. Not only do you need to learn vocabulary, syntax, and grammar, but you need to understand the various social contexts in which the language is spoken, gender differences, the cultural values reflected in the language, slang, euphemisms, and the subtle nuances of humor.

Despite how challenging learning a second language is for most Americans, there are many good reasons to justify the effort. First, learning a second language is absolutely essentially for developing rapport, trust, and long-term relationships with your foreign business associates. Second, learning a second language will make learning a third or fourth language considerable easier. Third, knowing a foreign language is good for your health, for, in the event of your becoming ill abroad, it is vital to be able to explain the nature of your illness to non-English speaking medical care-givers. Fourth, learning the local language can play a major role in adjusting to "culture shock" because efficient communication can (a) minimize the frustrations, misunder-standings, and aggravations that face the linguistic outsider and (b) provide a sense of safety, mastery, and self-assurance. And finally, as we have pointed out in this chapter, the best way to get "inside" a culture is through its language. By knowing how people categorize their world (which is what language does), you will gain a much fuller understanding of their values, attitudes, beliefs, feelings, and behavior patterns.

Cross-cultural Quiz (Answers on pages 203-204)

1. Bill Heller, an expatriate CEO of an American firm in the Philippines, hosted a retirement party for one of his Filipino managers. At such functions it is customary for colleagues and company leaders to give speeches praising the careers of the retirees. As CEO, Bill was the last to pay tribute to the retiring Filipino manager. Since the speeches had gone on for nearly an hour, Bill's speech was succinct, to the point, and very complimentary. However, Bill's speech was not very well received by either the retiree or the other Filipinos at the farewell party. What did Bill do wrong?

2. While making a sales presentation to a government agency in Peking, Victor Foster was asked about his company's overseas manufacturing facilities. He responded optimistically that they had operations in Brazil, Indonesia, and the country of Taiwan. For reasons that Victor could not understand, the meeting from that point on did not go well. The Chinese officials, who became increasingly non-communicative, eventually rejected the sales proposal from Victor's company. How do you explain this negative turn of events?

3. Manley Rosen, an enthusiastic fast-track executive with a manufacturing company from Memphis, was sent to Bangkok to set up a regional sales office. With the help of a local human resources consultant, Manley set up a number of

appointments to interview prospective employees. While his interviews with male candidates were reasonably successful, the female candidates were not responding very positively. In fact, the first several female candidates withdrew their applications after the first interview. Finally, and quite reluctantly, the local consultant gently told Manley what he was doing that was turning off the female candidates. What was it that the consultants told Manley that could explain this situation?

CHAPTER 6

NONVERBAL COMMUNICATION

When we think of human communication, it is usually language that first comes to mind. To be certain, all humans have language systems, which enable them to send and receive messages by putting words together in certain sequences. As important as language is to the communications process, humans also send and receive an enormous number of messages without ever uttering words. People communicate non-verbally in a number of important ways, including facial expressions, posture, gestures, touching, space usage, and eye contact.

Nonverbal communication often goes unnoticed because it is so much less obvious than language. In recent decades, however, nonverbal communication has been the subject of a number of scholarly studies. In their desire to show the importance of nonverbal communication for understanding other cultures, some scholars, no doubt, have gone overboard. One of the early authorities estimated that 93 percent of all human communication was nonverbal (Mehrabian:1971) A year earlier, Birdwhistle (1970) set forth a more modest estimate of 65 percent. It is legitimate to ask how in the world they came up with these precise percentages. Given the fact that the importance of nonverbal vs. verbal communication varies widely between cultures, such numbers have relatively little meaning. They represent a classic example of the "fallacy of the misplaced concreteness." That is, if we can ascribe a number, which appears to be very precise, then it must be accurate. Nevertheless, whether the nonverbal dimension of communication represents 93 percent or only 40 percent, the fact remains that nonverbal communication plays a significant role in human communication. Thus, in order to fully comprehend how people communicate in any particular culture, we must become familiar with both their nonverbal forms of communication as well as their formal language.

These two forms of human communication---language and nonverbal communication---must be viewed together because they are often interconnected and equally important to the communication process. Often nonverbal messages are sent alone, without any accompanying words. But more frequently, these nonverbal cues are sent along with words.

How do we send and receive messages without using words? Humans communicate nonverbally in a number of different ways. We communicate through "body language," such as gestures, facial expressions, posture, gait, body movement, and eye contact. We communicate by touching others or by withholding physical contact. Certain physical qualities of our bodies (such as body type, height, weight, skin color, and body odor) also convey different meanings in different parts of the world. We communicate by the artifacts we put on our bodies, such as clothing, make-up, perfumes, jewelry, and eyeglasses. Spatial distancing, such as conversational distances and seating arrangements, also send various messages. We even communicate by using time when we keep people waiting or arrive early to a party.

We frequently fail to realize how pervasive nonverbal communication is in our everyday lives. All cultures, for example, use *color* to convey various messages without actually using words. And, like other aspects of culture, the meanings attached to various colors vary considerably from one part of the world to another. Whereas in the United States the color blue is associated with masculinity and pink is associated with femininity, the French consider red to be the most masculine color while many cultures dress their little girls in yellow, not pink. Black is a funereal color in the United States, while the color white serves that same purpose in most Asian cultures. White symbolizes purity and virginity in the United States (thus, brides wear white wedding gowns), but in India brides wear red or yellow clothing. The color purple is associated with royalty in some countries and Easter in some Christian countries, but in parts of South America purple is the color of death. These variations in color symbolism are more than interesting tidbits of anthropological knowledge because they do have important implications for the conduct of global business. To illustrate, United Airlines got off to a shaky start when it initiated service to and from Hong Kong. As a way of welcoming their Asian customers, they gave them complimentary white carnations, only to learn afterwards that white flowers, which symbolize death and funerals, are not appropriate for festive occasions.

Words and nonverbal cues have a number of features in common. First, like words, nonverbal cues are learned from other cultural members. Second, both verbal and nonverbal forms of communication are symbolic (that is, an American learns that the words "I'm pleased to meet you" symbolize the same sentiments as the nonverbal cues of a handshake and a smile.). Third, nonverbal communication, like language, is arbitrary. There is, for example, nothing inherently rational about shaking one's head from side-to-side to indicate "no," for, in fact, that very nonverbal signal indicates just the opposite ("yes") in parts of India. And finally, both languages and nonverbal cues, as we shall see in this chapter, vary appreciably from one culture to another.

Despite these similarities between language and nonverbal communication, these two forms of communication are also different in some substantial ways. First, nonverbal communication has not been studied and documented as thoroughly as has language. While languages have been reduced to systems of syntax, grammar, and word meaning, scholars have not revealed the systematic nature of a culture's nonverbal communication. Second, whereas people explicitly are taught their language, a good deal of nonverbal communication operates at a much less conscious level. When speaking, we must carefully select our words; but our nonverbal cues are most often sent without any purposeful thought. And finally, some nonverbal messages, unlike words, are beyond the willful control of the sender. It is, in other words, often impossible not to communicate embarrassment when we blush, nervousness when we tremble or perspire, or fear when our pupils dilate.

Nonverbal forms of communication essentially serve four major functions. First, nonverbal cues enable us to repeat or reinforce our verbal messages. To illustrate, we can tell our spouse how much we love her while reinforcing those words with a kiss or a hug. Second, we can use nonverbal behavior as a substitute for words. Rather than verbally chastising an employee for coming late to work, a supervisor can give the tardy worker a "dirty look" that will be every bit as effective as a verbal scolding. Third, nonverbal cues can be used to control other peoples' behavior. For example, Americans can prevent someone from interrupting us in conversation by holding up a hand with the palm facing outward. And finally, nonverbal communication can actually contradict our verbal messages, as illustrated by the person who says that he is "fine" in an angry tone of voice. When nonverbal signs contradict the spoken words, we tend to believe the nonverbal signs.

Studies of nonverbal communication make many different distinctions between different forms. While we cannot examine how all of these modes of nonverbal communication vary cross-culturally, we will look at several modes in greater depth.

POSTURE AND STANCE:

How we stand, sit, or walk usually send either positive or negative nonverbal messages. If we stop and look at such behavior in our own society, we can observe a number of nonverbal messages being sent. Walking slowly and with stooped shoulders indicates a lack of assertiveness and self-confidence. A woman genuflecting in a Catholic Church is communicating submissiveness before her deity. A person holding his crossed-arms tightly against his chest probably is not looking for an intimate relationship. A person with his feet on his desk while talking to an employee is communicating informality and superiority. To turn your back on someone who is talking to you is an unmistakable sign of rejection. A hooker leaning seductively against a street lamp is advertising her services. And, the person who walks quickly, with an erect posture and with arms swinging, is likely to be a goal-oriented achiever.

While all of these postures are understandable within our own cultural context, we can send unintended messages with body language when operating cross-culturally. As discussed in Chapter Three, Americans tend to be highly informal in their social relations, preferring to minimize status distinctions and not wanting to "stand on ceremony." This basic cultural value is reflected nonverbally in peoples' posture. To assume an informal seated posture, many American males will sit with their ankle resting upon the opposite knee. While this is a perfectly respectable posture for American males in most social situations, it will be taken as highly rude and offensive by many cultures in the Middle East and Africa. Such a posture involves exposing the sole of the shoe, which, in those parts of the world, is considered to be the filthiest, most profane part of the body. In short, to show someone the sole of your shoe in the Middle East is an insult of the gravest magnitude.

Many middle-class North Americans, whose culture tends to de-emphasize status distinctions, have difficulty understanding how people in more formal cultures use posture and stance in social situations. Nowhere is body posture more important than in Japan, with its long tradition of bowing behavior. This very formalized posturing is essential for proper social interaction in Japan because it reflects the relative social status of the two people bowing to one another. The person of lower status, who is expected to initiate the bow, will bow more deeply than will the person of higher status. Bowing initiates conversations, it regulates the ensuing conversation, and it is used to bring the conversation to a close. Bowing is such an integral part of Japanese society that many banks and department stores employ professional bowers who greet customers at the door. And, the social custom of bowing is so ingrained into the Japanese psyche that people have been known to bow when greeting someone on the telephone.

HAND GESTURES

A very important form of body language is the use of hand gestures. Consider how many hand gestures we use every day to convey an idea without using words. We can wave "hello" or "goodbye." We can tell someone to "be quiet" by putting our index finger vertically against our lips. Without using words, we can petition someone to "speak up" by cupping our palm next to our ear. We can "thumb a ride" on the side of the road. We can register our approval or disapproval by giving a "thumbs up" or a "thumbs down." We can flash the "peace sign" by making a "V" with our index and middle fingers, or we can give "half of the peace sign," which conveys a very different meaning. Or, by making a circle with our thumb and index finger, we can signal that everything is "A-OK."

While all of these nonverbal signs are immediately recognizable by anyone reared in the United States, problems occur when we start to cross national boundaries. Take, for example, the last nonverbal sign described in the previous paragraph, the "A-OK" sign. While this sign carries a positive, up-beat message in the United States, it refers to money in Japan, zero (worthless) in France, male homosexuality in Malta, and is an obscene gesture (equivalent roughly to "half of the peace sign") in parts of South America. Thus, a single hand gesture carries with it at least five very different meanings in five different parts of the world.

This example of the "A-OK" sign illustrates how a single hand gesture has multiple meanings in different cultures. There are also many examples of the opposite phenomenon, namely, how different gestures in various parts of the world are used to refer to the same thing. To illustrate, in the United States the nonverbal way of referring to oneself is by pointing with the index finger to one's chest. Yet, when referring to themselves, the Japanese point to their noses, not their chest. Or, the nonverbal way of expressing admiration for an attractive women varies enormously throughout the world. To illustrate, the Frenchman kisses his fingertips, the Italian twists an imaginary moustache, and the Brazilian man curls one hand in front of the other as if to be looking through an imaginary telescope.

Like other aspects of language and culture, various nonverbal forms spread (or diffuse) from one culture to another. In a comprehensive study of nonverbal communication, Desmond Morris (1979) found that a number of hand gestures originating in Europe (and still prominently used there) have become widely used in the United States. For example, in both Western Europe and the United States, crossed fingers are used as a sign of good luck; thumbing of the nose is a sign of derision; and the "thumbs-up" sign indicates approval. Other nonverbal gestures, however, have not made a successful Atlantic crossing. To illustrate, Greeks, Spaniards, Frenchmen, and Italians use the *eyelid pull* (tugging on the lower eyelid with the forefinger) to signify "Be alert." People in the Southern Mediterranean area can tell you that you look "thin and ill" by using the *chin stroke* (gently stroking from the cheek bone to the chin with the thumb and forefinger). And, Italians can question one's masculinity by tugging on their own ear lobe, thereby sending the nonverbal message "I think you are so effeminate that you should be wearing an earring." The eyelid pull, the chin stroke, and the *earlobe tug* convey no particular meaning in the United States.

Not only do the details and meanings attached to hand gestures vary from culture to culture, but there is also considerable variation in terms of how prominent gestures actually are in any given culture. It has been suggested, only half jokingly, that Italians would not be able to communicate if their hands were tied behind their backs. While this is clearly an overstatement, the fact remains that Italians use hand gestures very liberally to emphasize and reinforce the spoken word. In a study of nonverbal displays among women on television game shows, Canadian women used fewer hand gestures than did women from the United States. Moreover, in Japan and other eastern countries, it is thought that adults who use too many gestures are childish and lack self-control.

TOUCHING

Touching is perhaps the most personal and intimate form of nonverbal communication. Humans communicate through touch in a variety of ways and for a variety of purposes, including patting a person on the head or back, stroking, slapping, kissing, punching, embracing, tickling, shaking hands, and laying-on hands. Every culture has a well-defined set of meanings connected with touching. That is, each culture defines who can touch whom, on what parts of the body, and under what circumstances.

Some cultures have been described as high-touch cultures and others as low-touch. Southern European,

Mediterranean, and South American cultures tend to be high-touch cultures, whereas such Northern European cultures as German and Scandinavian cultures and most Asian cultures tend to be low-touch. The difference between high- and low-touch cultures can be observed in public places, such as subways or elevators. For example, Londoners (from a low-touch culture) traveling in a crowded subway are likely to assume a rigid posture, studiously avoid eye contact, and refuse to even acknowledge the presence of other passengers. The French (from a high-touch culture), on the other hand, have no difficulty leaning and pressing against one another in a crowded Parisian subway. At least in the area of touching behavior, it is surprising that there can be such significant differences between two groups of people who are separated only by a narrow channel of water.

Perhaps the most common form of physical touching among global businesspeople is the shaking of hands. Yet, even here there is considerable variation is how people shake hands in different parts of the world. How often people shake hands, how much pressure is applied, and how long a hand shake lasts all varies considerable from one culture to another. The Germans, French, and Latin Americans shake hands frequently during the course of their encounters while most Asians shake hands quite infrequently. Americans and Germans like a firm grip when shaking hands while Arabs and most Asians prefer a light, gentle grip. Frenchmen shake hands quickly, while Arabs prefer a more lingering style.

Shaking hands can cause some particularly problematic situations when Americans travel to parts of East Africa or the Persian Gulf region. Frequently, North Americans, when wanting to emphasize their pleasure in meeting the other party, will reinforce the handshake by touching the person's right hand, forearm, or elbow with their left hand. While this is a nonverbal way of emphasizing friendliness in the United States, it can be highly offensive in the Arabic world, which has a strong prohibition against touching people with the left hand. In these parts of the world, the cultures distinguish between the right and the left parts of the body. The right hand, for example, is associated with sacredness and cleanliness while the left hand is seen as profane and filthy. Thus, even though the American is trying to be as friendly as possible, it is taken as an obscene gesture by the Arabic-speaker. It should go without saying that such different perceptions of the meaning of touching can have very negative consequences for building business relationships.

EYE CONTACT

Perhaps one of the most subtle and most salient modes of nonverbal communication is gaze or eye contact. It is, after all, where two people actually meet with their eyes. Even though certain aspects of eye communication is biologically based (such as communicating fear by dilated pupils), people are taught by their culture to use their eyes to send and receive messages. The many cultures of the world, thus, vary according to the degree to which each emphasizes maintaining or avoiding eye contact when communicating.

In North America, people are taught to maintain a considerable amount of eye contact when engaging in face-to-face communication. The meaning attached to this eye contact is attentiveness and respect for the other person. The amount of eye contact North Americans expect of one another, however, is not absolute. It is inappropriate to stare continuously at the other person. Instead, it is expected that we will maintain eye contact for several seconds, shift away momentarily, and then establish eye contact again. By world standards, eye contact in the United States is toward the high end of the scale. There are other peoples (such as Arabic cultures) that maintain a more intense gaze in everyday conversation than is found in the United States. Koreans and Thais maintain a moderate level of eye contact, while most other Asian societies avoid direct eye contact.

Problems in communicating across cultures develop because of different meanings associated with maintaining eye contact. As mentioned above, the meaning conveyed in the United States is attentiveness, interest, and respect for what the other person is saying. Unfortunately for the global traveler, this meaning is not only different in some other cultures, it is the *opposite*. Rather than being a sign of respect, most Asians interpret direct eye contact to be a hostile, threatening gesture. Most Asians show respect by avoiding eye contact, not holding it. Japanese, for example, tend to focus their eyes somewhat below the eyes, around the region of the Adams apple. This difference in the meaning of eye contact has caused misunderstandings when Asians and Americans are attempting to communicate with one another. The American thinks that the Asian, by avoiding eye contact, is being inattentive, disinterested, and even rude. Asians, on the other hand, will feel browbeaten by what they consider to be a threatening stare. In fact, Asians often experience a similar level of discomfort that North Americans feel when they are speaking with Middle Easterners, who maintain a very intense gaze in normal conversation.

In some parts of the world, people cannot hold a conversation without maintaining a fairly high level of eye contact. This, of course, presents a problem when two people are expected to talk while simultaneously walking, side-by-side, down the street. Usually, this is not a problem for most North Americans, who adjust to maintaining less eye contact in such situations. Italians, however, are uncomfortable with not being able to look into each other's eyes when conversing. Richard Gesteland illustrates this point from a personal experience that he had while conducting business with an Italian colleague in Florence. While traveling down the highway at 85 miles per hour, his Italian colleague, Giorgio (who was driving) was briefing him on the complexities of the negotiation scheduled for later in the day. According to Gesteland (1999:73),

Giorgio. . . wanted to be sure I understood every single detail. So he kept studying my face intently to see if I was getting it while waving his free arm to emphasize the importance of what he was telling me. I couldn't believe it. Here we were, hurtling around curves and roaring through dimly-lit tunnels at high speed in a car driven one-handed by a guy whose eyes were focused more on the passenger next to him than on the road ahead.

DISTANCING

One of the least understood modes of nonverbal communication is known as proxemics, or how different cultures define space. Largely through the pioneering research of Edward T. Hall, we now better understand how people communicate through the use of personal space. How close two people stand to one another in normal conversation tells a lot about their relationship. And that distance, to a very considerable degree, is determined by a person's culture. To illustrate, most middle-class North Americans generally get no closer than approximately 20-22 inches from each other's mouths in normal conversation. Some cultural groups, such as Scandinavians and Northern Germans, typically distance themselves about 30 inches. But many other cultures in South America, North Africa, and the Middle East need considerably less space than North Americans. For example, whereas North Americans keep 20-22 inches from each other, people from parts of South America keep 14-15 inches, and Kuwaitis and Saudis get as close as 9-10 inches from each other in normal conversation. In fact, in some parts of the Middle East, you would be considered to be aloof, remote, and standoffish if you could not feel the warmth of the person's breath with whom you were conversing.

It should not be difficult to imagine the type of misunderstanding that could occur when an American and a Saudi meet for the first time. After their initial greeting in the lobby of a hotel, the American wants to establish a personal distance of 20-22 inches from the Saudi's mouth, but the Saudi feels more comfortable with a distance of 9-10 inches. The American takes one step backward to re-establish his comfort zone. The Saudi counters by taking a step forward in order to re-establish his. This little "dance" (with the American stepping backward and the Saudi stepping forward) continues for the next several minutes until the two men find themselves at the opposite end of the hotel lobby. And all the while, what are these two culturally naive men thinking? The American is thinking to himself, "Why is this guy threatening me? Is he making a sexual advance on me? Is he trying to intimidate me?" The Saudi, on the other hand, is wondering to himself, "Why is this American running away from me? Doesn't he like me?" Unfortunately, both the American and the Saudi failed to understand the powerful effect that space has on the dynamics of our cross-cultural communications.

This scenario involving spatial distancing between the Saudi and the American is noteworthy because it is played out in many parts of the world. These various (culturally produced) notions about space represent a very subtle aspect of culture. But, how do North Americans learn to get no closer than 20-22 inches from others? And, how do Puerto Ricans, Germans, and Indonesians acquire their notions of appropriate distancing? We certainly don't learn it in school or read it in books. How many Americans can remember being told by their parents, "Now, remember, never get closer than 20-22 inches from someone else's mouth!" Even though proxemics is not part of our formal (or even conscious) education, we all learn from our cultures what is appropriate space usage. And, as members of our particular cultural group, we learn it very effectively and adhere to it very consistently.

People bring their culturally defined notions of space to the workplace. This can be seen from how people behave when traveling to their office. In the United States most people commute to their place of employment in their own automobiles. People prefer their own individual space (their own cars) rather than being cramped into some form of public transportation. On the way from the parking lot to the office, many Americans find themselves on a crowded elevator. Whenever Americans are forced into spaces which compromise their 22-inch space bubble, they compensate for the loss of space by certain predictable behaviors. For example, when confined in a crowded elevator, Americans naturally stop talking, face the front of the elevator, assume a fig leaf position (purses and briefcases hanging down in front of the body), and keep their eyes fixed on the floor indicator panel above the doors. If a nudist should enter the elevator and face the other riders, most Americans would not acknowledge the nude's presence, but instead would continue to stare at the floor indicator panel.

Once in the American workplace, we can see how the very ecology of the office is influenced by the North American notion of space. Each person has his or her own space in which to work. Private offices with doors and walls carry more social status than cubicles with partial walls. Offices with windows are occupied by more prominent people than are interior offices. Offices on the upper floors are more desirable than offices on the lower floors. And, of course, large offices are reserved for those with the greatest power and status. High-level people in the organization have their personal space (which is large, windowed, and on the top floor) well protected by doors and secretaries. Moreover, they will sit behind large desks, designed to ensure that the "unwashed masses" keep their proper distance.

While sharing many features with the ecology of the American office, space is defined in Germany with even more emphasis on hierarchy and the preservation of privacy. German offices are designed to insure maximum privacy. All offices have heavy (solid core) doors, which are almost always kept closed. The American expression "My door is always open" has little meaning in Germany. Accustomed to sitting behind a desk separating them from their business associates, Germans become uncomfortable when someone moves his or her office chair closer to the desk. In fact, Edward Hall, the father of cross-cultural proxemic studies, reports (1966:137-38) that "a German newspaper editor who had moved to the United States had his visitor's chair bolted to the floor 'at the proper distance' because he couldn't tolerate the American habit of adjusting the chair to the situation." By way of contrast, French office workers share workspace in a large open area. Frequently the boss will sit in the center of the non-partitioned workspace, surrounded by his subordinates, and with the most recently hired located at the periphery.

CONCLUSION

A full understanding of patterns of nonverbal communication is absolutely essential for meeting one's professional objectives in the new global economy, whether you are managing, negotiating, or advertising your products abroad. In the area of global advertising, for example, we cannot simply export our successful advertising campaigns from home and expect them to meet with equal success in foreign markets. Time and again we have seen how advertising in non-American markets should reflect the *local* culture and its communication patterns rather than one's own. For example, a recent study by Kim (1998) has documented significant differences in nonverbal forms of communication in magazine advertising in the United States and Korea. More specifically, Kim found that Korean models in magazine ads were less expressive in terms of smiling, displayed fewer arm and hand gestures, had less eye contact, and were less often touching one another than were their American counterparts. The study concluded that the much greater emphasis on nonverbal communication (smiling, gesturing, eye contact, and touching) among the American models in magazine ads would not be effective in Korea because they ran counter to Korean cultural values.

Our discussion (above) of the various modes of nonverbal communication, segmented neatly into sections on posture, gestures, eye contact, etc., might lead us into a false sense of security. Nonverbal behavior does not lend itself to easy description or neat categories. Even within a single cultural/linguistic community, there is likely to be a number of internal variations based on gender, age, religion, or social class. To illustrate, many of the generalizations concerning Arab nonverbal behavior were made by observing business-men and male students. It is not at all likely that these same generalizations would hold for Arabic women, whose communication patterns and general lifestyles are more constrained and private. Or in the area of hand gestures, Japanese women hold a hand in front of their mouths when laughing or smiling. But, this polite gesture is found only among Japanese women, not Japanese men. It is, therefore, advisable to exercise some caution when generalizing even within a single linguistic community.

As we have pointed out repeatedly in this chapter, all people communicate without words, there are many different modes of nonverbal communication, and the actual details of nonverbal communication vary enormously from culture to culture. Mastering the realm of nonverbal communication becomes even more challenging when we realize that there are some cultures that tend to emphasize nonverbal communication over language. U.S. culture, for example, places greater importance upon the spoken word, while many eastern cultures, the Japanese in particular, look to nonverbal messages as a primary conveyer of meaning. North Americans, therefore, are likely to underestimate the import-ance of nonverbal cues in a global business setting. As important as language is in all human communication, it is imperative that as globally savvy players in the new millenium we learn to "hear" the silent messages and "read" the invisible words of nonverbal communication wherever we may encounter them.

Cross-cultural Quiz (Answers on page 204-205)

1. While working on a six-month assignment in her company's Taipei office, Kathryn Skye made arrangements to meet for dinner a classmate from the Harvard Business School. While enjoying the food and getting caught up on each other's lives, the Taiwanese classmate, who currently works for a large software company, tells Kathryn about his plans for starting his own software consulting business. Unfortunately, he needs to wait before he launches the business because he is unable to get the proper telephone number for the business from the telephone company. Given all of the work he has done to write his business plan, it strikes Kathryn that a telephone number should not delay the opening of the business. But Kathryn's former classmate insists that he cannot start his new enterprise until he has the right telephone number. How can you explain to Kathryn what is going on?

2. On a month-long business trip to Thailand, John Culligan, the vice president for marketing for a Pittsburgh chemical company, was invited to the home of one of his Thai business associates. Upon arrival, John shook hands with his host and hostess as well as with their Thai maid who had answered the door. John was startled when the maid burst into tears and made a hasty retreat to the kitchen. He didn't have the foggiest idea what he had done to cause such a negative reaction. How can you explain this unanticipated turn of events?

3. Mike Hutchison, a hardware engineer for a leading U.S. computer company, was working at the Tokyo facility and had a chance to meet with one of Japan's leading computer scientists. Mike asked him about his latest research project, which he proceeded to outline in considerable detail. Although fascinated with the description of the project, Mike became increasingly annoyed because the Japanese computer expert kept pausing to ask if Mike understood what he was saying. Mike began to think that the Japanese scientist thought he was too stupid to understand. What is going on here?

CHAPTER 7

GLOBAL COMPETENCIES

In our introductory chapter, we mentioned that the process of developing global brains involved the acquisition of new knowledge *as well as* the mastery of a number of new skills and competencies. In the preceding five chapters, we have concentrated on the knowledge base needed to become a global player in the 21st century. We have looked at the concept of culture, a model for understanding comparative cultural values, and varying ways by which people in different parts of the world communicate with one another. In a sense, that is the easy part of developing global brains because it involves the acquisition of knowledge---something we have done throughout our formal education. This section of the book, however, will be considerably more challenging because it will involve altering your mindset, some of your fundamental philosophical principles, and in some cases, the way you behave. You will, in other words, be expected to manage your own "paradigm shift," based on new ways of thinking, rather than relying on your old familiar set of ideas.

For much of the 20th century, before the process of globalization started to pick up speed and intensity, leaders within an organization were able to get along with a fairly traditional mindset. The distinction between a *traditional mindset* and a *global mindset* (the latter of which is absolutely essential for success in the 21st century) has been discussed by Rhinesmith (1992, 1996) and Brake, Walker, and Walker (1995), among others.

Traditional Mindset	Global Mindset
Narrow perspective based on functional area	Broad, cross-functional perspective
Contradictions to be prioritized	Contradictions to be balanced
Conflicts are to be eliminated	Conflicts seen as opportunities
Problem-solving through hierarchies	Problem-solving through networked processes
Individual mastery/competence	Teamwork is emphasized
Resist change/change seen as a threat	Create change/change seen as an opportunity
Master specific knowledge/skills	Emphasis on life-long learning

Many of the skills and competencies needed for the new millenium are derived from those in the right-hand column. Whether we like it or not, we will need to move from those pre-dispositions on the left to those on the right. Some readers, particularly those at the beginning stages of their careers, may already be operating according to the principles of the global mindset. For those of you who are, then you will need to re-enforce those ways of thinking and acting into the future and throughout your careers. For those of you who are still looking at the world through your traditional frame of reference, your task will be more formidable. But, the good news is that you *can* develop a global mindset. For some it will be arduous, for others even daunting. But you may be surprised at how pleasant, rewarding, and growth-producing the process will be. If you go into it with a positive attitude, you just may find that learning to re-orient your world-view can be both recreational and educational. And remember, you are not expected to complete the entire paradigm shift overnight. It really is something you need to be working on throughout your lifetime. Here, then, are the basic elements of the global mindset that accompany global brains.

1. Develop a broad perspective: Unlike the more traditional domestic manager, the global manager needs to develop the broadest possible perspective. The emphasis should be on seeing the big picture. This involves a type of "systems" thinking whereby one can see how the various parts are interconnected to make a systematic whole. Even manufacturing companies that see themselves primarily as domestic operations are comprised of a number of parts, such as machines, people to operate the machines, customers, suppliers, accountants, distributors, maintenance personnel, sales people, and many layers of managers, to mention just some. All of these parts of the company are intimately interrelated to the extent that a change in one part is likely to bring about changes in other parts. Thus, to develop a broad perspective means seeing the organization through a wide-angle, rather than a telephoto, lens. It involves developing one's peripheral vision so as to better see how all of the parts of the system operate. The person with a broad perspective is never satisfied with a single explanation of an event. Instead, the person possessing a global mindset is constantly scanning the whole complex system to look for less obvious root causes that are found in more distant, yet interconnected, parts of the system. And, of course, as our organizations become more global, the parts of the system (and their relationships) become increasingly more complex.

Unfortunately, westerners in general, and Americans in particular, have not had much experience with systems thinking. Most adult Americans operate with a fairly mechanistic view of the world. That is, our world is comprised of organizations, which like complex machines, are made up of a number of parts. Our natural tendency is to focus on the parts rather than the whole system. When a problem occurs, we attempt to solve it by taking the "broken machine" apart in order to locate the defective part. We divide our world into isolated, insolated sectors that take on a life of their own. Our colleges are divided into units based on academic disciplines; our medical professions are so highly specialized that dermatologists have very few opportunities to share their medical information with obstetricians; and our private companies are usually rigidly divided according to functional areas, such as production, marketing, and accounting.

Within the last several decades, however, the western world has been experiencing a profound shift away from this mechanistic type of thinking and toward a mindset that focuses more on how all of the parts work in relation to the whole. This major paradigm shift can be seen in the new ways that organizations are being restructured and realigned. Our private businesses are now entering into all sorts of new alliances with their customers, their suppliers, and even their competitors. And, the old organizational charts, with their hierarchical ordering of discrete units (usually represented by boxes) are now giving way to organizational networks, which tend to emphasize relationships between boundaries.

The broad vision needed to understand the integrated nature of an organization is well illustrated by Rick Ross (Senge, 1994:108-9.) Ross gives an example of the plant foreman who sees the interrelationships of the parts of an organization by asking a series of probing questions. While walking through the plant, he notices a puddle of oil on the floor. When he asks a nearby worker why there is oil on the floor, he is told that an overhead piece of machinery is broken. "And why is it broken?," the foreman queried? "Because," he is told, "it has a faulty gasket." Probing further, he asks "And why is the gasket defective?" "Because," the worker explains, "the purchasing department got a good deal on gaskets." As it turned out, the purchasing department, responding to upper management's demand to cut costs, purchased the least expensive gaskets, thus causing the oil puddle on the plant floor. Thus, a policy made at the highest levels of management affected how supplies were purchased, which, in turn, caused the machine to leak oil on the plant floor. Now, if a plant worker slips on the oily floor and hurts himself, the accident could be traced, at least indirectly, to a policy created by upper management. The plant foreman, through his series of probing questions, is demonstrating the type of systems thinking needed to gain a broad perspective on the problem.

Along with a broad perspective, global leaders need what Wills and Barham (1994:50) refer to as "cognitive complexity," comprised of the twin abilities to differentiate and integrate. Differentiation involves being able to see how a single entity is comprised on a number of different parts; integration, on the other hand, involves the capacity to identify multiple relationships between the different parts. The truly complex thinker---an essential trait for success as a global leader---is the person who can engage in both types of thinking and can move comfortably between the two. The cognitively complex global leader, in other words, feels comfortable moving from the specific parts to the whole and back again. In terms of the organizational structure, the successful international manager has the ability to focus on the unique needs of the local situation while at the same time maintaining a good grasp of how it fits into the overall operations of the parent organization.

Even if you are part of an organization that sees itself as primarily a domestic operation, your need for a broad perspective is no less important. This "systems" type of thinking is absolutely necessary if you are to continually scan for potential markets, suppliers, workers, and customers. Moreover, if you are not looking at your profession from a global perspective, you are likely to be blind-sided by foreign competitors who will enter, and likely take over, your domestic markets. Thus, having a broad, global perspective is absolutely essential, irrespective of whether you are operating domestically or all over the world.

Developing a broad perspective, in a sense, involves thinking "outside of the box," or beyond the rather narrow scope of one's functional area. Or perhaps a better way of putting it is that it involves "expanding the size of your box."

To be certain, knowledge of your functional area is important and should not be neglected. But the global mindset involves going beyond, way beyond, the confines of one's functional responsibilities or immediate job description. You can capture the big picture by expanding your vision to include the worldwide forces that are impacting upon your products, suppliers, customers, and technologies. Having a global mindset means never being satisfied with the amount of information at your fingertips about the global economic, political, and social forces that are impinging upon your job and your organization. Systems thinkers are constantly asking themselves a number of important questions:

- How can I find out about the best practices in my industry from all over the world?
- How can I convince others in my organization to seriously consider adopting some of these best practices that could make our organization more competitive?
- How is my own job related to other jobs in the organization, both domestically and abroad?
- What professional publications do I need to read on a regular basis so as to track the major trends in my functional area and my industry?
- What professional organizations do I need to join in order to keep abreast of the global nature of my job, my profession, and my industry?
- How can I continually expand and maintain my personal and professional relationships throughout the world so as to gather timely and relevant global information?
- What is the most efficient/effective way of sharing my global knowledge with others in my organization?

These are just some of the questions that people interested in developing a broad perspective must ask themselves---and then answer as completely as possible.

2. Balance contradictions: A major requirement for being an effective global manager is to be able to balance contradictory needs and demands rather than prioritize or attempt to eliminate them. Contradictions and conflicts should be seen as opportunities, not as liabilities. Conflicting values, behaviors, and ideas are a fact of life in the world today, and they are not diminishing in number. The world is not becoming culturally homogenized into a single monolith. If anything, the cultures of the world are becoming increasingly more diverse and insistent upon maintaining their unique identities. One needs only to look at such ethnic conflicts in Ireland, the Middle East, and the former Yugoslavia, among many others, to realize that people are willing to die to preserve their precious heritage and ways of doing things. Or as Thomas Friedman (1999:30) reminds us, the Norwegian people in a 1994 referendum chose *not* to join the European Union because to do so would require giving up too much of their Norwegian identity and way of life. So, despite the rapidly growing number of people that are becoming electronically inter-connected these days, we are not likely to witness a sudden outbreak of cultural homogenization. Thus, differences (and conflicts) in the workplace will certainly be the order of the day in our work lives and beyond.

The key word in this global competency is balance. Most positions of leadership, and particularly those in truly global organizations, place many contradictory demands on our performance. Your boss may request you to improve responsiveness to your customer needs, but such an alteration is likely to increase your costs. Or some of your staff work more productively in a competitive setting while others prefer a higher level of cooperation and collaboration. The natural tendency for most westerners is to prioritize the contradictions and then eliminate them by deciding on a course of action favoring one over the other. But, the globally savvy leader needs to be able to co-exist with, learn from, and manage the never-ending contradictions found in any global organization, rather than trying to resolve them in any definitive way. The rationale behind balancing, rather than eliminating, contra-dictions is *synergy*---that is, the notion that by debating the contradictory or even conflicting ideas, perspectives, and positions, you will eventually arrive at a far better solution to the problem when a decision is finally made.

The typical traditional mindset attempts to eliminate all contradictions by establishing and adhering to a rigid set of corporate policies designed to create discipline and efficiency. Yet, while this "one size fits all" approach provides a measure of security for the traditional corporate manager, it also limits creativity and a more flexible decision-making process. The global mindset, on the other hand, does not try to eliminate all conflicting situations by relying on a standardized set of corporate principles, irrespective of the circumstances. By balancing tensions and contradictions, the global leader is essentially embracing duality. By acknowledging that totally different solutions might be called for in different parts of the world, they are more likely to be successful in the world of global business. As Black, Morrison, and Gregersen have suggested (1999:97), the new global leader of the 21st century sees corporate policies much like a suspension bridge, stable enough to cross, but sufficiently flexible to accommodate changing conditions. In other words, a rigid set of policies cannot be implemented uniformly throughout the world. The global leader must know when to follow the policies, when to bend them, and when to ignore them altogether, all for the benefit of the organization.

Unfortunately, North Americans, and many western Europeans, are not particularly adept at balancing contra-dictions because it flies in the face of some of our basic cultural pre-dispositions. In our study of comparative values earlier in this book, we described North Americans as action-oriented, pragmatic, and concrete rather than contemplative, philosophical, or interested in analyzing the intricacies of a problem. For most Americans, the emphasis is on solving the problem, biting the bullet, and making a decision as quickly as possible. Conflict and complexity are things to be managed, overcome, and put out of the way so progress can be made. And since North Americans generally believe that they can control themselves and their environment, then they tend to see contradictions and conflicts as things that can be wrestled to the ground, conquered, and eventually eliminated. This very practical (and typically American) approach to conflict stands in stark contrast to how contradictions are dealt with in some other parts of the world. In Asia, for example, the world is perceived in terms of dualities or binary oppositions, which, they believe, are natural and the very essence of life itself. The Chinese see life always fluctuating and changing between two ideal poles, the yin and the yang. This type of ebb and flow of contradictory/conflicting elements is seen as a natural part of the universe, not something that must be stabilized by selecting one pole and eliminating the other.

In order to have global brains, we must learn to think more like Asians than like traditional Americans. In every workplace, we are confronted with a number of polarities that really defy resolution. Do we centralize our operations or do we de-centralize them? Do we try to expand our market share by offering the best quality product or the product at the lowest cost? Do we base our decisions on hard-core information or on more subjective intuition? Do we retain all decision-making power in the hands of those at the top, or do we delegate it to a much wider group? Do we organize our workforce cooperatively or competitively? Do we solve problems by deconstructing them or by analyzing them in a holistic fashion? These are just some of the contradictions our business leaders of the 21st century need to learn to balance. They need to understand that neither option is inherently right or wrong, nor will one predominate over the other in the long run.

Learning to balance complexity is no easy matter. Nevertheless, there are a number of things you can do today that will give you valuable practice at identifying, analyzing, and managing complex global relationships. The more aware you become of complexity, the more comfortable you will be with it, and the more adept you will become at coping with it. First, you can develop a system for assessing the nature of the complexities of your organization. This involves establishing an on-going dialogue with other players in the organization. Second, it is imperative that you never stop looking for opportunities to decentralize certain decision-making processes while centralizing others. For example, you might find that the research function of your organization requires centralized control and a uniformity of approach, while sales, marketing, and customer service should be decentralized so as to maximize local responsiveness. Third, unless you are constantly aware of the nature of the contradictions in the workplace, you will never know how to exploit them for the sake of making the best possible decisions. And finally, one way to become comfortable working with a never-ending set of contradictions is to take a course in conflict management.

3. Be curious: A prerequisite for developing a broad perspective is an insatiable appetite for new knowledge. Of course, you can force yourself, through sheer will power, to master the big picture, but you will do it quicker, more completely, and more pleasantly if you are naturally inquisitive. Before you can balance the many contradictions facing today's global leaders, you must develop a wide-angle view of (a) global similarities and subtle local differences and (b) the complex networks that exist between varying parts of your own organization. Grasping this enormous complexity requires the non-stop asking of questions and seeking of answers. It is for this reason that curiosity lies at the heart of developing global brains.

Being naturally curious is absolutely essential because it drives you to seek relevant information needed to make good decisions. But often the sheer magnitude of the information is so daunting or complex that you must draw on your inquisitiveness again to ask additional questions in order to make sense of the information. Once your curiosity has led to asking relevant questions, gathering relevant data, and analyzing those data, then you are ready to make decisions and embark on a course of action. It is, of course, possible to be so inquisitive that you never stop asking questions and get around to making decisions. The globally savvy person is the one who continually asks questions but knows when to finally bite the bullet and use the information to actually take action. And even if the course of action is taken without all of the facts (which is often the case), the curious person will continue to ask questions, gather data, and if need be, make on-going adjustments to action plans already in operation.

Curiosity makes the globally savvy business person adventuresome. When traveling abroad, the person with a global brains doesn't spend his or her free time in a western style hotel where everyone speaks English. He walks the streets, smells the scents, listens to the sounds, watches people playing out their lives, takes the initiative to meet new people, all the while systematically observing what is going on. He reads local newspapers rather than relying on the International Herald Tribune. He watches locally produced newscasts instead of CNN. These inquisitive leaders immerse themselves in the local culture, not because they want to become more interesting cocktail party conversationalists, but rather because what they learn will enable them to more effectively meet their professional objectives. That is, their curiosity will pay big dividends by providing knowledge about new markets, technology, cultural values, customer preferences, and the human side of the local workforce.

Being inquisitive really involves living one's life *purposefully* and *experientially*. You don't start off your day by asking yourself how can you best get through the day with as little effort as possible. Rather, you start the day by asking yourself, "What can I learn today?" Not only do you want to learn but you want to learn experientially. The globally savvy person is much like a cultural anthropologist doing fieldwork. In many cases, anthropologists---whose job it is to learn as much as possible about the culture---cannot rely solely on library accounts about the culture. They have no choice but to study the culture through what they call "participant-observation," living among the people while at the same time making systematic observations about the culture. Of course, the more the cultural anthropologist *experiences* the culture, the greater the learning will be. Whether you are an anthropologist or not, the process is the same. By throwing yourself into a new cultural environment, you will have a venue for your curiosity, and you will glean all sorts of new information. And, by constantly comparing and contrasting this new information with what you already know, you will be developing critical insights into developing new strategies and courses of action.

Being inquisitive involves a totally different mindset from what is typically found in the western world. When most people seek out the answer to questions, they frequently are too willing to accept information that simply confirms what they already know. Truly inquisitive, and globally savvy, people start off from the assumption that they don't know what is true, but they want to know. They have, in other words, a realistic understanding of how little they understand. The good news is that they truly believe that they can acquire the needed information by asking the right questions. In fact, knowing how to ask the right question can often be as important as the answer itself.

A major obstacle to learning through curiosity is the typically American affliction of thinking that you know more than you actually do. All too often Americans simply assume that people from other parts of the world have nothing to offer them. But this type of cultural superiority complex can be self-defeating. Howard Perlmutter of the Wharton School of Business reminds us that when Americans enter into a joint venture with a Japanese firm, the Japanese will send many people to the U.S. to learn everything we know, while we send one person to Japan to tell them everything we know (Kupfer, 1988:58). But the globally savvy person does not have an overly optimistic view of his or her own knowledge. Instead, he or she knows that culturally different people may, and often do, have perspectives that can be informative and valuable. And, it is the curious person who will ask the tough questions, even when the answers may challenge his or her own strongly held views.

4. Build relationships: In our earlier discussion of comparative values, we made the point that Americans, as well as many western Europeans, tend to emphasize individualism over collectivism. While individualism and a fiercely independent mindset are hallmarks of the successful capitalist, they can be problematic when operating on the global playing field. Outside of North America, Australia, the British Isles, and parts of Western Europe, people from most other parts of the world place a much higher value on creating and maintaining long-term social relationships in all aspects of their lives, including the conduct of business. Westerners, on the other hand, concerned as they are with not wasting time, are primarily interested in conducting business based on the merits of the transaction. They place relatively little value on getting to know one's business partner personally or building rapport. They don't feel that they need to have a personal relationship built on trust with their business partners. The most immediate need is to "do the deal." Problems arising after the contract is signed can always be worked out by the lawyers. Thus, Americans and western Europeans see no pressing need to build strong <u>personal</u> relationships with their business partners, and as a result, are not very good at it.

The single biggest challenge for westerners looking to become globally savvy is to learn how to build meaningful personal relationships with foreign customers, employees, suppliers, and business partners. This involves a considerable expenditure of time, which, unfortunately, most westerners believe is in limited supply. It also involves an ability and a willingness to connect emotionally with people whose languages, values, and expectations may be vastly different from one's own. As difficult as it is for most westerners, it is absolutely essential if you are to learn about new potential markets, know how to meet your customers' needs, mentor future employees, or learn how to adapt company policy to local situations.

Building and maintaining solid relationships is good for both individuals and organizations, particularly in today's fast-paced business world. With the recent trend toward mega-mergers, former competitors are now partners seeking to expand their markets and profitability. Organizations are forming tighter linkages with their suppliers, vendors, and retailers. And with an increasing number of stakeholders, it seems all the more important to build solid relationships founded on trust. Even though the process of building relationships can be time-consuming, it should be viewed as an important investment. The benefits may not seem obvious in the short run, but over time they can pay significant dividends.

Most successful global players are successful because they like people and are good at building relationships. In many countries outside of Western Europe and the United States, the creation of strong, emotionally based, relationships are a prerequisite for conducting any type of business. Unfortunately, there are no absolutely fail-safe ways of building such relationships. They take time, nurturing, and a lot of emotional energy. The process of building meaningful connections starts with a genuine interest in other people. You must demonstrate through your actions that others (both within and outside of your organization) are important to you *as people*, not just as cogs in the wheel of business. You should expect to engage in a lot of "non-business" socializing, such as dining, drinking coffee, playing golf, or attending cultural events. Remember, others need to get to know you, to understand your character, and to be able to trust you before they can become your customer, client, or loyal employee.

Knowing how---and being willing---to build strong relationships enables us to achieve value-added results. Only through relationships are we able to help others meet their full potential. By taking the time and energy needed to build relationships, we are eliciting the skills, talents, and perspectives of others. When this happens, our personal and professional lives are enhanced. In short, it enables us to do more and better things.

We can learn something about building relationships with culturally different people from cultural anthropology, the discipline that studies contemporary cultures all over the world. One generally valid piece of advice for any cultural anthropologist doing fieldwork is to proceed slowly. Don't, in other words, attempt to ask the local people highly specific questions from day one. However, the typical western cultural anthropologist, whose own culture greatly values time, does not take kindly to the suggestion of slowing down. Since his time is limited, he feels that he must make the best use of his time. His natural tendency is to "hit the ground running" and collect as much data as possible. However, always having an eye on the clock can be counterproductive because the very quality of one's data depends on laying some social groundwork.

The successful anthropological fieldworker needs to spend time and emotional energy establishing his credibility by allowing the local people to get to know him. As an anthropological fieldworker in Kenya in the 1970s, this writer spent the first three months (of an 18 month-long field project) engaged in a number of activities that did not relate to the business at hand, that is, collecting cultural information. Before I started to ask systematic questions, I spent many hours helping people with their income tax forms, showing teenagers how to shoot a 15-foot jump-shot, or taking people for rides in my car. All of these "non-productive" activities served to demonstrate that I was interested in them as people, rather than merely sources of information. Once the local people got to know and trust me, they were far more willing to give me the type of cultural information I was looking for.

Building relationships cannot happen unless you are willing to show respect to those with whom you are working.

A major stumbling block to the process of making personal connections is an overly inflated ego. Sometimes aspiring global players have such an exaggerated sense of their own importance that they refuse to connect emotionally with culturally different people. This is particularly true when the people are in lower status positions. If you are smitten with your own sense of superiority, it is not very likely that you will be able to emotionally connect to others or gain their trust. If you are not genuinely interested in getting to know other people, they will know it soon enough. Interest and respect are not things you can fake.

A particularly effective way of demonstrating your genuine interest in relating to people is to put yourself in a subordinate role, such as student, rather than that of the teacher. If you have a real interest in getting to know someone, you must be willing to let them talk about themselves, their jobs, and their culture. After all, they *are* the experts on those subjects. In all likelihood, you will begin to gain their trust by simply listening to what they have to tell you. By being genuinely interested in what they have to say, you will be facilitating the relationship. After all, you are taking an interest in their favorite topic of discussion, themselves. Who could possibly fault you for that?

In addition to assuming the role of learner, there are many other things you can do that will convey an interest in building long-term relationships. When entertaining foreign business partners at home, flying their flag in front of your headquarters would be viewed as a generous gesture of friendship, hospitality, and good will. Or, rather than entertaining your foreign guests in an expensive restaurant, they might be pleasantly surprised if you organized a special dinner featuring food from their country. These gestures, while small, will go a long way in conveying to your foreign business partners that you care about their way of life, and by implication, that you care about them.

5. Be perceptually acute: Successful leaders of the 21st century need to be perceptually acute in a number of ways. They need to be able to accurately derive meaning from their interactions with people from a wide variety of cultures and subcultures. This involves being attentive to both verbal and nonverbal communication, deriving meaning from social context, and being sensitive to the feelings of others and to one's effect on others. The best way to develop this skill is to practice analyzing cross-cultural scenarios (similar to the ones found at the end of chapters 2-7 of this book) in which communication between people from different cultures breaks down. This requires that you focus on alternative explanations rather than relying on explanations that might seem logical or obvious from your own cultural perspective. One has to consider not only the words exchanged in these scenarios, but also the nonverbal cues, the social context, and the assumptions embedded in the other culture.

Active listening is at the heart of being perceptually acute. Hearing and listening are two quite different processes. Unless we are physically impaired, we all hear the words of others. But hearing, which involves receiving sound waves as stimuli, is a passive process. Listening, on the other hand, requires our active attention, interpretation, and understanding of those stimuli. A recent survey of American executives revealed that 80 percent of those surveyed believed that listening skills were among the most important for corporate leaders, even more important than technical skills. (Salopek, 1999:58). Unfortunately, this same survey revealed that the skill of active listening was one of the weakest skills in the American workforce. As we have mentioned elsewhere, our communication style tends to emphasize speaking rather than listening.

While most Americans are not very good listeners (and very few have ever taken a course in listening), it is a skill that can be learned if you have the time and motivation. The skill of being an active listener can have dramatic effects on your success as a global player. First, listening is the best way to gather information. And, to be certain, we need to get our hands around an increasing amount of information these days. If we can just learn to keep our mouths shut and not attempt to dazzle people with our brilliance, we will receive all the information we need. And, the beauty of it is that others will be doing most of the work! Second, becoming an active listener helps build meaningful, long-term relationships. By listening, you create an audience. In other words, when you listen to others, it is much more likely that they will listen to you. Others will reason that if you are smart enough to listen to them, then you must have something that is worth listening to. Third, you will create greater rapport with people by becoming an active listener. Listening, in other words, will enable people to trust you more. And when that happens, people are more likely to listen to you without having to convince them to do so.

Developing good listening skills may be easier said than done. Nevertheless, there are some general guidelines that, if followed, can help you receive oral messages more effectively.

- Be aware of the phenomenon that psychologists call *cognitive dissonance*, the tendency to discount, or simply not hear, any message that is inconsistent with what you already believe or want to believe. In other words, if the message does not conform to our preconceived way of thinking, we subconsciously tend to dismiss its importance. It is important to give yourself permission to actively hear all messages—those that you agree with and those that you don't. It is not necessary that you agree with everything that is being said, but it is important to hear and understand the message so that you will then be in a position to seek creative ways of resolving whatever differences may exist.
- Listen to the whole message before offering a response. Focus on understanding rather than interrupting the message so that you can give a rebuttal/response. Because

no one likes to be cut off before he or she is finished speaking, it is vital for the effective listener to practice allowing other people to finish their ideas and sentences.

- Concentrate on the *message* rather than the *style* of the presentation. It is easy to get distracted from what is being said by focusing instead on how it is presented. No matter how inarticulate, disorganized, or inept the speaker might be, try to look beyond those stylistic features and concentrate on the content of the message. It is often little things, like a gesture or a turn of phrase, that can turn us off and cause us to be distracted. It would be helpful to identify those things that cause us to lose focus, so we can learn to take them more in stride.

- Learn to ask simple, non-threatening, open-ended questions, designed to allow the speaker to elaborate on a particular point. Avoid close-ended questions, which will usually only give a "yes" or "no" response. Open-ended questions, on the other hand, will provide much more information, such as who, where, what, when, and how.

- Be conscious of staying in the present. We all try to listen with a wide variety of baggage from the immediate past. It is tempting to start thinking about yesterday's racquetball game with a friend, this morning's intense conversation with your boss, or the argument you had with your spouse at breakfast, but to do so will distract you from actively listening to what is being said.

- It is important to be conscious about *not* becoming bored. The average human mind is able to process about six hundred words per minute. Since people can speak at only about 120 words per minutes, our minds have a lot of time to wander. When this happens, we lose our focus and can no longer concentrate effectively on the hard work of listening.

- In most cases, it is advisable to check back with the speaker to make sure that you really understand what is being said. This involves paraphrasing back to the speaker what you think he or she is saying. If it is correct, then it will confirm your understanding. If it is incorrect, it will provide a second chance to get it correct. In either case, it conveys to the speaker that you are working hard at listening to what is being said.

- Be aware of the nonverbal cues (such as body language, intonation, and facial expressions) being conveyed by the speaker. Sometimes these nonverbal cues contradict the words that are being spoken. When there is a discrepancy between the words spoken and the nonverbal cues accompanying the words, it is likely that the nonverbal signals are a more accurate reading of how the person actually feels.

- Don't forget to give feedback to the speaker. Everyone needs to feel as though he is being understood. A committed listener lets the speaker know that he is receiving the message by periodically uttering such phrases as "Oh really," "O.K.," "Go on," or "Is that right?" Keep in mind how good it feels when others affirm that they understand what you are saying. So, don't be overly frugal with your feedback.

- In almost all situations, taking notes will help you become a more effective listener. Provided you don't attempt to record every word, selective note-taking can help to highlight what is being said. Not only will note-taking help to document the messages, but when the speaker notices that you are taking notes, he or she will, in all likelihood, make a special effort to be clear and accurate.

6. Develop flexibility: On most lists of competencies for global leaders is the need to be flexible, non-judgmental, and open to new ways of thinking and explaining phenomena. Flexible people are able to adjust easily to different people, approaches, and situations and can revise their game plan quickly as circumstances dictate. This means, essentially, that the individual is willing to learn and postpone making evaluations until more facts are known. Such a capacity involves the suppression of one's ego and the letting go of old paradigms when the situation calls for it. In a very real sense, global leaders must experience a psychic transformation, which entails letting go of cultural certainty and being willing to see the internal logic of another perspective. This type of flexibility is not just a nice thing to have, but it actually enables us to understand our own culture and those of others, mobilize diverse people, serve diverse clients and customers, and operate across cultures with maximum success. Only by remaining open and flexible will it be possible to understand why culturally different people act and think the way they do.

Being sufficiently open and receptive to new ways of thinking is particularly important as we enter the 21st century with its constantly changing environments. The speed and complexity of change in the world today is often staggering. People who have mastered technical competence in a number of professional areas are often overwhelmed by feelings of uncertainty caused by this rapid change. And, it is this very uncertainty that requires us to remain flexible and respond quickly to changing situations. Sometimes we need to make decisions without having all of the necessary information at our fingertips. Thus, the global leader, who remains flexible and does not suffer from "hardening of the categories," views rapidly changing environments as *opportunities*, rather than threats.

Some observers have likened the global marketplace to white-water rafting, an activity requiring considerable flexibility. If we are to navigate the rapids successfully, we must respond quickly to the constantly changing contour of the waves. If we remain overly rigid, it is likely that we will find ourselves outside of the raft. As Napolitano and Henderson (1998:24) remind us:

> *Without flexibility we become like a stick caught against a rock in a turbulent stream; defenseless against the force of the raging water, the stick is battered relentlessly. A stick that floats free, on the*

other hand, moves with the water rather than against it and is carried along unencumbered; thus the force of the water actually expedites the stick's progress along the way.

The need for remaining open and flexible has been well illustrated by Foster (1992:254–55), who tells of a U.S. businessman trying to sell data processing equipment to a high-level government official in India. After preparing himself thoroughly, the American was escorted into the official's office for their initial meeting. But much to the American's surprise, seated on a nearby sofa was another gentleman who was never introduced. For the entire meeting the host government official acted as if the third man was not there. The American became increasingly uncomfortable with the presence of this mystery man who was sitting in on the negotiations, particularly as they discussed specific details. After a while, the American began having paranoid delusions. Who was this man listening in on these private discussions? He even imagined that the man might be one of his competitors. The American negotiator became so uncomfortable with this situation that he lost his capacity to concentrate on the negotiations and eventually lost the potential contract. Here was a perfect example of a negotiator who was unsuccessful because he could not adjust to an unfamiliar situation. In India, as in some other parts of the world as well, it is not unusual for a third party to be present at negotiations. They may be friends, relatives, or advisors of the host negotiator invited to listen in to provide advice—and perhaps a different perspective. Unaware of this customary practice in India, this U.S. negotiator began to imagine the worst until it had destroyed his capacity to focus on the negotiations at hand.

It is important to keep in mind, however, that flexibility does *not* mean losing sight of your basic principals and objectives by chasing after every new fad that comes along. You still must have your own personal and professional goals, objectives, and moral/ethical positions. In these highly volatile times of the 21st century, these core principles and goals are as important as ever before, and we should make every effort to let people know that they are nonnegotiable. But flexibility is important because there may very well be more than one route to your destination. In other words, a bridge without some flexibility will never withstand the force of an earthquake.

7. Be able to shift paradigms: The mark of any competent leader is the mastery of the basic truths about how the world operates. Leadership involves, in other words, doing your homework, learning a lot of facts, distinguishing the important from the less important variables, seeing interconnections between phenomena, understanding the major generalizations that hold true about our personal and professional lives, and finally, being able to communicate those truths to others. While this mastery is a necessary prerequisite for competent leadership, it is not sufficient. The truly competent leader of the 21st century also needs to be able to let go of these "absolute" truths in light of new evidence to the contrary. To be certain, these truths have been internalized only after a great deal of hard work and emotional investment; they have been painstakingly explained and taught to others; and they have been woven into the very fabric of a person's life. But, today's leader needs to be sufficiently open to the possibility that these truths may be temporary. One must be willing to revise his or her "absolute truths" to accommodate new findings, ideas, and insights. He or she must avoid being tied to existing ideas and practices solely because they have held true in the past.

In some cases, these "absolute truths" are so big and important that they provide us with a general model of what is real and how we should behave. These models, or paradigms, are extremely useful because they give order to our lives and provide guidelines for our behavior. While these paradigms are useful, they can entrap us if we accept them uncritically. If we are not open to testing our assumptions and looking out for new evidence, our paradigms can blind us to how the world is changing. When we are too rigidly tied to our existing paradigms, we are not in the best position to take the most appropriate course of action.

An example of a paradigm shift occurred in the United States government in the mid-1980s. For much of the 20th century, and particularly since the end of WWII, the United States was a world leader in the area of manufacturing, including automobiles, steel, appliances, electronics, heavy machinery, and agribusiness. The government saw our nation's economic health as being dependent upon the acquisition of natural resources, maintaining a skilled industrial workforce, and protecting our markets from foreign competition. During the 1970s and 1980s, however, a number of other countries throughout the world began to expand their industrial bases, thus cutting into our market share of products ranging from automobiles to Levis. At the same time, the world was on the verge of entering the information revolution, whereby ideas, information, and intellectual properties were becoming as important to our economic well-being as the manufacturing sector. Seeing and understanding this trend (which accelerated in the 1990s), Congress altered the structure and mission of the Office of Copyrights. Prior to the mid-1980s, the Register of Copyrights essentially oversaw the office that provided exclusive legal rights to authors, musicians, software developers, artists, and others for developing their intellectual and artistic properties. As such, the Register of Copyrights was a civil servant whose work was in Washington, DC.

But in the mid-1980s, the role of the Register of Copyrights changed dramatically. Congress essentially had a paradigm shift, away from envisioning the US economy as being primarily based in manufacturing to one whose long-term existence depends on the world-wide protection of our intellectual properties. Since the 1980s, the Register of Copyrights has spent much more time outside of the United States, negotiating treaties with foreign governments and bringing them more in line with our copyright laws. The idea here is that our continued economic growth into the 21st century depends on our being able to *sell* Microsoft Word, Britany Spears CDs, and John Grisham novels to the Koreans, rather than having them bootlegged. Thus, seeing the changes that were beginning to take place, Congress had the foresight to alter its model of reality (i.e., paradigm), and take a significantly different course of action.

We can, no doubt, recognize a number of changes in our immediate business environments in the recent past that have required serious paradigm shifts. The practice of being tied to a particular desk in a particular office now seems like a thing of the past for many workers, who now work at home or from temporary work stations in the central office. The move from writing on yellow legal pads to the use of networked computers, which surely involved a significant paradigm shift, has altered dramatically how information flows both within and between organizations. Or, the recent inclusion of day care facilities, owned and operated by large corporations, illustrates a major change in the way corporate America views both workplace satisfaction and worker productivity. These are all changes in the workplace that have required a substantial shift in our models of reality. Irrespective of whether we like them or not, they do indicate how significant changes can only happen when people are willing to shift paradigms and view things in new ways.

8. Act with integrity: As we enter the 21st century, we find a world that is becoming more fast-paced, heterogeneous, and complex. If we are to succeed in such a world, we will need to build and nurture relationships built on mutual trust. There is nothing particularly complicated about building trust, nor are there any simple shortcuts. Trust only comes by acting with integrity---which means keeping promises, being honest with yourself and others, avoiding hidden agendas and game-playing, and accepting full responsibility for your actions. Acting with integrity involves standing behind your words and commitments no matter how convenient it might be to do otherwise. Trusting relationships occur only when others can count on your words and actions. In short, integrity is the bedrock on which trusting relationships are built.

Integrity is something that develops from an early age. When one is growing up, it always helps to have strong role models (parents, teachers, and friends) who have strong morals and are willing to act on them. But it is never too late to develop integrity. No matter how often we may have compromised our integrity for the sake of convenience or personal gain, our integrity can be reclaimed, provided we are willing to ask ourselves some hard questions. What are our non-negotiable core values to which we are willing to commit? Have we sold these values out in the past? Quite apart from what may have happened in the past, are we really willing to stand behind these values in the future? Are we willing to monitor the extent to which we are tempted to stray from our core values? If we can focus on doing the right thing (rather than simply doing things right) by acting on our principles, we will be acting with integrity. Sometimes acting on our commitments may not seem to be in our best interest. But, in the long run, people will notice and learn to trust us. And when they do, we have built the foundation for trusting relationships.

A large part of integrity within a business context involves acting in accordance with your espoused values. Nothing can be more discouraging than to have your boss or leader say one thing and then behave completely differently. To illustrate, the company president may speak eloquently about the need for diversity within the workplace, but then willfully fails to take action against those discriminating against women or Hispanics. Or, take the sales manager who urges his staff to listen to customer feedback, but then refuses to act on this information. In these and other cases that readily come to mind, there is a "disconnect" between what a person says and what he/she does. Some of these cases can involve blatant hypocrisy. But, more often than not, there is usually a gap between our words and our deeds. The challenge that faces our leaders of today is to eliminate that gap to as great a degree as possible. If they do not "walk the talk" (that is, act in accordance with their stated values), then they will not be taken very seriously by those they are attempting to lead. People need to know that their leaders will not compromise their stated values for the sake of expediency. In short, they need to be shown that their leaders are operating with integrity.

Acting with integrity often takes courage because it requires that you act on your principles, even though it might not be particularly popular to do so. Cooper and Sawaf (1996:167-168) relate a powerful story about one such case. A consultant working on motivational issues with a leadership team of a successful corporation found, much to his surprise, that the level of energy was extremely low. After some pointed questioning, the consultant learned that for years the leaders of the corporation had engaged in "creative bookkeeping practices" verging on illegality. This willful complicity with less-than-ethical accounting practices was sapping the energy and vitality of these high-level leaders. They had been playing "fast and loose" with their ethical principles, and they were beginning to pay a high emotional cost. The consultant's recommendation, to voluntarily submit their books to an IRS audit, while hardly popular, was designed to atone for their collective loss of integrity so they could again feel good about doing their jobs. Even though the CEO was stunned by the recommendation, he eventually had the good sense to follow it. After the company paid several million dollars in back taxes and penalties, the deadening psychological burden had been lifted and high levels of energy returned to senior management. Here was an example of how the forfeiture of integrity (i.e., engaging is semi-legal or downright illegal business practices for the sake of material gain) reduced the self-esteem, self-confidence, and motivation of their organizational leaders.

Acting ethically and with integrity is the right thing to do, but it is also good business and good for your career. Business leaders are constantly tempted to compromise their integrity in a number of areas, including bribery, abusive labor practices, product safety, and environmental degradation. To simply look the other way in the face of injustice or wrongdoing is often justified because you might benefit in the short run. To do the right (ethical) thing could cost you or your company money or put you in disfavor with your superiors. But in the long run, acting with less-than-full integrity will be counterproductive for both the individual and the organization she/he represents. In other words, compromising your integrity today is likely to come back to haunt you down the road by undermining your long-term relationships with customers, employees, and governments. This is surely what financier Warren Buffett had in mind when he told a group of MBA students at Brigham Young University in 1996:

> *When looking for managers, I basically look for three things: integrity, intelligence, and energy. The problem is that if they don't have the first, the other two will kill you. Why? Because if someone doesn't have integrity, you really want them to be dumb and lazy. It is only if they have the first, that the second two really count. (Quoted in Black, Morrison, and Gregersen, 1999:141)*

9. **Become emotionally resilient**: Leadership in the 21st century requires that you have the capacity to deal with adversity in constructive ways and can bounce back from it quickly. No matter how well you plan a course of action, there is always the chance that it will not happen according to plan. Even worse, sometimes awful things happen to good

people for no apparent reason. We are all susceptible to frustrations, disappointments, and even tragedies, but those who are emotionally resilient have the capacity to deal with them and get on with their jobs and their lives. Emotionally resilient people are confident about their ability to deal with ambiguity, have a generally strong self-concept, have a good sense of humor, and generally have a positive outlook on life. They like to confront new experiences, are not afraid to take risks, nor are they overly concerned about making mistakes.

Now that we are actually in the new millenium, the need for emotional resilience is greater than ever before. Things rarely go as planned when living and working in our fast-paced and heterogeneous world. Frustrations are frequent and stress is high. While unanticipated problems occur in any leadership situation, they occur with greater regularity when operating in an environment in which the rules are imperfectly understood. Thus, working in the global arena becomes a cauldron or training ground for learning how to deal with unanticipated problems, frustrations, and stress. In order to succeed as a global player, it is imperative that the international manager learn to bounce back rapidly after disappointment or frustration. This involves rejecting feelings of self-pity and martyrdom in the face of adversity by maintaining a positive, up-beat attitude. Thus, practicing effective stress-reducing techniques is essential for becoming an effective global leader.

The global leader does not try to avoid adversity. He or she knows that adversity happens, and when it does, it is the person's ability to rebound from adversity that distinguishes the leader from the non-leader. In fact, the saying that "adversity builds character" is not simply a post-facto mantra to help us get through rough times. Adversity does, in fact, build character, provided, of course, you have emotional resilience. Adversity is character-building because it is responsible for our most important learning experiences. If we think back on those occasions when we really learned some of life's most important lessons, it was during times of disappointment, frustration, crisis, or even tragedy. Those lessons probably were not learned in a classroom, but rather when we had the wind knocked out of us and didn't have any past experience to fall back on. Learning, in other words, takes place when we somehow manage to overcome a crisis, face tragedies, and eventually get beyond our disappointments, heartaches, and frustrations. The secret is to deal constructively with the negative turn of events, maintain one's personal and professional equilibrium, and come out stronger than before.

We all know personal stories of people who displayed emotional resilience during times of trouble. Most people of note have encountered rough times. They had to face daunting odds, innumerable obstacles, and many failures before winning a certain measure of notoriety. What set these people apart is how they handled the adversity. They refused to be defeated. They faced their crises with courage, creativity, and determination; learned something by reflecting on them; and then pulled themselves together to try all over again. Perhaps Winston Churchill said it best when he defined success as "going from failure to failure without loss of enthusiasm."

Unfortunately, we also are aware of people who show little or no emotional resilience whatsoever. These are the people who are not usually described in books. They have difficulty approaching unfamiliar situations with a positive attitude. They spend far too much time blaming themselves or (even worse) others for their misfortunes. They avoid having new experiences, trying new things, meeting new and different people, or eating new foods for the first time. They have difficulty laughing at their own failures or mistakes. They express relatively little confidence in their coping skills. Generally, they take an unusually long time to get over their disappointments and failures, and when they do, they seem unwilling to try again. In other words, they often react to adversity by going to bed, assuming the fetal position, turning the electric blanket up to "9," and not coming out for three months.

Emotional resilience---which is so essential for today's leaders with global brains---is well illustrated by an incident that occurred to French President Charles de Gaulle and his wife. While being driven in the suburbs of Paris, President and Madame de Gaulle had their car fired on in an assassination attempt. The car was riddled with bullets, glass was shattered everywhere, and the driver nearly lost control of the car. After the car came to a halt, President de Gaulle got out of the car, brushed the glass off of his clothing, and observed, "They are really bad shots." Here is emotional resilience in action. After nearly being killed, de Gaulle displayed an optimism and sense of humor that enables him to bounce back from adversity.

10. Be personally autonomous: Another important competency of the successful global leader of the 21st Century is personal autonomy. To be open, flexible, and nonjudgmental does not entail adopting the thoughts and behaviors of others as one's own; nor do you even need to like them. But while remaining open-minded (so as to learn more about other perspectives), you must not abandon your own identity in favor of theirs. Personal autonomy involves having a sufficiently well-developed sense of self so as not to be threatened by culturally different people or to abandon one's own identity in favor of theirs (that is, "going native"). Having a strong sense of who they are and what they value, they are not overly dependent on cues from others. Valuing their cultural roots, they come to the international arena as mature adults.

When people become global players by traveling around the world, their new environments (people, business practices, customs, and values) do not provide the same type of external reinforcement that their home culture provides. This becomes a problem for those who are not personally autonomous because they are overly dependent on environmental cues for their own identity. When their egos are not reinforced by these environmental cues, they begin to feel lost, almost like non-persons. But for the person that is truly personally autonomous, they can maintain a sense of self because their identity is reinforced internally, not externally. Their personal values are based on their own beliefs rather than a blind conformity to the standards of others. Thus, they are open to exploring other cultures and perspectives, but they are well-grounded in their own.

Robert Rosen, author of Global Literacies, discusses Zhu Youlan, CEO of a Hong Kong-based company, who is the very embodiment of personal autonomy. Zhu Youlan is a strong leader who takes her rich Chinese cultural heritage very seriously. She not only has accepted the responsibility of passing on her cultural heritage (which she learned from her elders) to future generations, but she has a deep understanding of how her cultural roots influences, and even guides, her thinking and behaving. She brings to the bargaining table a healthy knowledge of her culture (with all of its strengths and shortcomings) and is willing to share that knowledge with others. As a global leader who displays a strong sense of personal autonomy, she has an honest sense of who she is in the world, as well as the influences her culture has had on her and her business. Because she is so grounded in her own Chinese culture, she is confident and mature. She suffers from neither cultural superiority nor cultural inferiority, and, as such, she can be open to under-standing the values and perspectives of others without having to betray her own.

Being personally autonomous has a number of advantages. People with personal autonomy are able to interact with different people without fear of losing their own identity. Because they are well-grounded in their own cultural values, the autonomous person can engage in cultural self-criticism and can also profit from feedback from others without becoming overly defensive. This personal autonomy also allows a reasonable response to failure, which is seen more as a learning experience than as a blow to their self-image. Moreover, a strong ego enables people to better handle stress, which can reach particularly high levels when operating abroad. Those people with little personal autonomy are likely to revert to more dysfunctional stress-reducing devises, such as alcohol or drugs.

Ten Competencies for Global Brains:

- Develop a broad perspective.
- Balance contradictions.
- Be curious.
- Build relationships.
- Be perceptually acute.
- Develop flexibility.
- Be able to shift paradigms.
- Act with integrity.
- Become emotionally resilient.
- Be personally autonomous.

Cross-cultural Quiz (Answers on page 205)

1. While paying a courtesy call on a corporate client in Argentina, Charles Lott decided to bring him a small gift, a Swiss Army knife he purchased while on a recent business trip to Switzerland. After receiving the present, however, the Argentine client seemed upset and not at all appreciative. What went wrong?

2. Rod Mackillop was sent to Hong Kong to set up a new office for his company. He had made arrangements to spend several days with a Chinese colleague to look at office space

with a realtor. However, after two full days of looking at a large number of properties, Rod's Chinese colleague has had something negative to say about all of them. Rod became frustrated because he was not sure how long he would have to stay in Hong Kong. How do you explain this situation?

3. In an attempt to open up its marketing outlets in Europe, a large manufacturing firm from Dallas sent one of its young executives, Michael Wagner, a recent MBA from Stanford University, to present its product line to a reputable distribution company in Munich. Michael was particularly well-suited for the task because he spoke fluent German, had worked in Germany for several years, and was an articulate spokesman for his company's product line. During his 90-minute presentation to the German company, he did all of the right things, including speaking in German, giving a firm handshake to the German executives, and making a logical sales presentation. But his sales presentation was not particularly well-received, and in fact, the German company chose not to distribute Michael's products in Europe. What went wrong?

Epilogue

Global Brains has explored the knowledge base, on the one hand, and the competencies, on the other, that you will need to become a successful global player in the 21st century. This is not your typical self-help book which promises to take ten strokes off your golf score, beat the stock market, or buy a million dollars worth of real estate with no money down. That genre of book promises---some even guarantee---a specific outcome if you follow their sure-fire, never-miss, no-think strategies. The alleged outcomes are all very specific and easily quantifiable. That is, readers will either take ten strokes off their golf score or they won't. This book, however, makes so such grandiose claims. We don't promise to get you a raise, a better job, or a pile of money in a matter of weeks. Rather, we are suggesting that if you (a) understand and apply the concepts and insights from Chapters 2-6 and if you (b) master the competencies discussed in Chapter 7, you will, over the long run, become a more successful player in the global economy in the 21st century.

It is important to keep in mind that there are no magic pills that will stimulate the growth of global brain matter. It involves hard work, diligence, and the capacity to embrace change rather than fleeing from it. It is imperative that you understand what it is that you want to do with your life and career. Before embarking on a quest for global brains, you really need to follow the advice of the ancient Greeks---that is, "know yourself." To be certain, some people simply do not have the desire, inclination, or temperament to become global players. Stuck in their traditional ways of thinking, they prefer not venturing outside of their own safe little world. But, the very fact that you have gotten this far in the book is a strong indication that you are powerfully motivated to become a world class player, one who is personally aware, socially skilled, and cross-culturally competent.

A dominant theme running through this book is the powerful, yet often over-looked, effect of *culture* on our everyday lives. Not only are there thousands of cultures in different parts of the world, but we operate here at home within a web of cultures and subcultures, including school cultures, church cultures, ethnic cultures, and corporate cultures. These cultures strongly influence the way we think and behave, and they often are radically different from other cultures. By understanding and appreciating the nature of cultural differences and similarities throughout the world, we will prepare ourselves for operating in a world that is rapidly losing its borders. Thus, the systematic study of culture is an indispensable tool for the successful global businessperson.

Developing global brains is a life-long process. It is not something you either have or don't have. Rather, a global mindset is always "in process," provided, of course, that you remain aware of the knowledge base, continue to hone the competencies, and become a life-long learner. Moreover, all of us are at different stages of developing global brains. For some, becoming globally savvy feels natural and, consequently, progresses at a rapid pace. Others, who are more resistant to change, experience more difficulty letting go of their old ways of thinking and doing things. Some of us grow their global brains best through formal training programs, while others learn best through personal experience. The good news, however, is this: Wherever you may be at the moment in your personal quest for global brains, there is no one who cannot continue to improve, become more savvy, and thus more successful at meeting your personal and professional objectives as a resident of the global village.

Having global brains involves a new set of attitudes, behaviors, and skills that will help today's global leaders become more personally, socially, and cross-culturally aware. In some cases, these pre-dispositions and competencies are not just different, but, in fact, the opposite, of those that have held leaders in good stead in the past. Today's global leaders can no longer work to eliminate conflicts, but instead need to balance contradictions and see them as opportunities. In a world that is becoming increasingly borderless, today's leaders can no longer rely on personal self-awareness and individual mastery alone, but rather must be cross-culturally astute and capable of managing culturally diverse teams of people. This capacity to bring people with different perspectives together will produce *synergistic relationships*, which are capable of accomplishing more by working together than any one could accomplish individually. Moreover, effective leaders for the 21st century need the ability to manage change continually and the uncertainty that accompanies it. Rather than seeing change as a threat, today's global leaders need to flow with change, see the potential opportunities in the change, and, in some cases, actually bring about change themselves.

Perhaps the most challenging aspect of developing a global mindset involves becoming empathetic---that is, being able to put yourself into another person's shoes. This term, no doubt, strikes the traditional leader of the 1970s and 1980s as overly "touchy-feely." Yet, to be an effective leader in the 21st century, it is imperative that you develop the capacity of understanding others in terms of *their* cultural assumption rather than your own. When encountering a behavior or an attitude that seems strange or even offensive, the best way to make sense out of it is to look at it from its original cultural context. It involves letting go of the absolute certainty that your own ways of thinking and acting are inherently correct, while all others are flawed. To act with empathy does not (I repeat, *does not*) require that you comprise your own culture in any way. It doesn't require that you take on their behavior or their thoughts as your own. You don't even have to like them. But, by being empathetic, the globally savvy person benefits in a number of ways. She or he will be able to *understand* the rationale behind the thought or behavior, will be able to better meet the other person's needs, and in the process, mostly likely will meet her or his own personal and professional goals.

Prior to the "Age of Information," which began to gain momentum in the 1990s, jobs were typically divided into a number of repetitive tasks that were spelled out explicitly in a "job description." While some jobs today still entail a set number of specific tasks (e.g., working on an assembly line), many jobs are becoming much more fluid, requiring employees to solve a number of different problems that keep changing. These jobs call for a different type of employee, one who can move comfortably from project to project and capable of solving a wide number of new and changing problems. Such jobs require non-stop learning. Because of the rapid pace of change in the Information Age, employees need to rely less on their resumes and more on their ability and willingness to master new information and skills.

When we speak of life-long learning, we are referring to learning in a number of different ways, including formal class-work, on-the-job training, mentoring, reading, formal and informal feedback, computer-based learning, and reflection. Moreover, the subject matter is also wide-ranging and varied. We need to keep abreast of new technology, new developments in our field, and the newest and most relevant processes affecting our organizations and employees. Whatever the method and the content might be, however, the most important idea is that learning is an ongoing, never-ending process.

Despite the fact that continuous learning is absolutely essential for today's leaders, there are several forces that tend to undermine the need for life-long learning. First, our formal educational system leads us to believe (erroneously) that after completing our BA, MBA, or PhD degree, we are "educated," and thus, finished with our learning. Second, American corporate culture generally assumes that once you are in a leadership position, you have put in your time, earned your stripes, and consequently, are capable of handling any problems that come along. Thus, the job of the leader/manager involves leading and acting, not learning and reflecting! And third, corporate America's preoccupation with the bottom line (i.e., high productivity and cost-cutting) is counterproductive to encouraging life-long learning. Rather than affording time to examining and learning about the big long-term structural features of our organizations, we expect our leaders to concentrate on such trivial and short-term matters as next month's sales projections. After all, corporate leaders are evaluated on their bottom-line results. As a result, leaders are not encouraged to study and reflect upon the larger issues of long-term trends, the long-term effects of work force diversity, or the cultural dimension of their overseas operations. Instead "learning" within the organization is relegated to a list of training sessions periodically offered by the human resources department.

True leadership requires that we overcome these disincentives to learning. Instead, we need to embrace a learning mindset. This involves some skills already mentioned in other sections of this book, including developing your curiosity and becoming an active listener. First and foremost, however, it involves being a purposeful and proactive learner. You cannot be satisfied with simply allowing educational experiences to wash over you. Instead, you need to be very purposeful about what you want to learn, how you will learn it, and how you will know that your learning is valid. Moreover, excellent leaders are not only good learners, they are also good teachers. The same desire that makes you want to learn should be harnessed to enable those around you to learn. To be certain, your own excitement for learning will be contagious and you will inspire by example. Yet the leader must also be purposeful about creating an environment where people can not only learn, but can learn collaboratively. This involves structuring a learning environment where people, ideas, and technology all come together.

It is relatively easy to call for life-long learning as a prerequisite for leading in the 21st century. It is considerably more challenging to know how to do it. The process of learning involves more than the collection of facts and experiences. Those facts must be pondered, reflected upon, and analyzed in order to understand them fully. That understanding takes a quantum leap forward when we begin to see how the facts are interrelated, that is, how they fit into a relatively coherent system. While all people have different ways of learning, below are some suggested guidelines for becoming a life-long learner.

1. Learn to ask "knock-your-socks-off" questions. These are questions that dig below the surface of a problem and often challenge conventional assumptions.

2. Disabuse yourself of the notion that to ask questions demonstrates ignorance or weakness. The only way to learn is to ask more questions than you answer.

3. Learn with a point of view. In other words, your learning should be disciplined and informed by a point of view (albeit one that is being modified over time), rather than a random, shot-gun approach to data gathering.

4. Be very deliberate about building learning time into your workday rather than leaving it to chance. In addition to your "to do" list, you might want to have a daily "to learn" list.

5. Continuously test your own assumptions and perspectives by engaging people who are different from you. Your purpose is to create as many contrasting ideas, interpretations, and perspectives as possible. If this makes you uncomfortable, take heart because you are probably learning something. This is the only way of knowing the best course of action during rapidly changing times.

6. Engage yourself in frequent introspection about the nature and appropriateness of your positions, assumptions, and perspectives. Sometimes our strongly held positions can actually prevent us from perceiving and understanding some areas of learning.

7. Despite the fact that some may see it as "non-productive time," find a regular time and place for reflection. You will find that this is the best time to ponder those things learned, see how the parts fit together, and see how they can be applied.

8. When learning, take the long view. It is impossible to learn everything you need to know in a short period of time. In fact, since our professional lives are changing at such dizzying speeds, we have no idea today what we will need to know two years from now. But getting the big picture, which is complex and multifaceted, usually comes in bits and pieces. It takes time to see how today's learning relates to what you learned last week and what you might stumble upon tomorrow. So be patient.

Today, to a greater extent than any time in history, our future success depends on our ability to learn and grow. We never know all there is to know. Rather we are all "becoming," or as some would say, "a work in progress." New challenges, which are surfacing every day, require new tools, new insights, and new strategies. So, life-long learning is essential if we are to be effective leaders into the future. Yet, at the same time, continual learning has the additional benefit of being self-renewing. Peter Senge (1990:14), author of the Fifth Discipline, suggests that learning allows us to regenerate ourselves by becoming creative, enabling us to do new things, and allowing us to perceive our relationship to the world. So often we spend year after year doing our jobs, over-extending ourselves, becoming stressed out, and eventually depleted. By focusing on doing our jobs and leading our lives, we often overlook the need to replenish ourselves, to recharge our batteries, or to refill our reservoir of creativity and new ideas. And yet, if we fail to renew ourselves through continual learning, we will become stale, uncreative, and ineffective.

APPENDIX

Answers to cross-cultural quizzes found at the end of Chapters 2-7

Chapter Two

2-1. What Mary failed to understand is that in Bolivia purple flowers are used only for funerals. Since the color purple is associated with death, purple flowers should be avoided as gifts in Bolivia.

2-2. In China, the expression "He wears a green hat" conveys the meaning that a man's wife or girlfriend has been unfaithful. Clearly no self-respecting Chinese male would want to walk around wearing a green hat. Ted's choice of green for the color of the hats was an unfortunate one.

2-3. The candidate is demonstrating a presentation style that the French are accustomed to and respect. The French prize eloquence and knowledge of history and literature as a means of conveying that one is a cultured, well-educated person. The inclusion of these types of references would be a normal part of a well-executed presentation in France. This knowledge of French culture, however, should never be a substitute for product knowledge and technical expertise.

Chapter Three

3-1. In many South American countries, to be corrected in public is bad enough, but to be corrected in front of a subordinate is particularly humiliating. By being primarily concerned with the task of instructing his foreman, Arthur failed to understand the dynamics of the situation, and therefore, caused the foreman to lose respect in the eyes of his subordinate.

3-2. Victor failed to realize that in Japan it is bad luck to receive four of anything because the number four is associated with death. As a result, Japanese avoid the number four. This is particularly true when giving gifts. When in Japan, give three or five of an item, but not four.

3-3. In Colombia, gifts are not immediately opened because Colombians do not want you to think they are greedy. It is also common for Colombians not to acknowledge the gift. But, just because they may not have verbally acknowledged the gift does not mean that it was not appreciated and treasured.

Chapter Four

4-1. Because of the very egalitarian nature of Australian society, single riders in a taxi are expected to ride up in the front seat with the driver. Even high-paid executives or government officials riding in a limousine are seen riding up front with the chauffeur. For a single passenger to ride alone in the back seat of a taxi makes many Australians uncomfortable because it symbolizes a large gap in status and prestige between the passenger and the driver.

4-2. Renee had actually caused two cultural gaffes. First, in Malaysia the head is considered to be the most sacred part of the body, the seat of one's spiritual power. While patting a child on the head is a very affectionate thing to do in North America, in Malaysia it is seen as a violation of the most sacred part of a person's body. Second, many Malaysians believe that to compliment a child on their beauty is to bring bad fortune upon the child. If evil people and spirits think that a child is gifted or beautiful, it is believed that they will want to harm the child. Thus, Malaysian parents will discourage you from complimenting their children so as to protect them from harm.

4-3. Unfortunately, Ralph made two basic mistakes. First, senior executives in Belgium usually get to the office later in the morning than do their subordinates. By going in early, Ralph created an awkward situation among his staff members, who weren't sure how to react when their superior came in early in the morning. And second, Belgians tend to be private and reserved. Office doors are usually kept closed and people knock before entering someone else's offices. Forcing Belgians into an "open-door" policy would therefore make them feel awkward and uncomfortable.

Chapter Five

5-1. Unlike most Americans (who tend to be very verbal), Filipinos generally are uncomfortable making public speeches. Thus, at such occasions as retirement parties, one way of showing appreciation to the honoree is to give not only a flattering speech, but a long one. The longer the speech, the greater the tribute because the speaker is expressing his/her willingness to subject themselves to a high degree of discomfort and embarrassment. Bill's choice to be brief and to the point was actually interpreted by the Filipinos as disinterest and a lack of appreciation for the retiree.

5-2. The Chinese bureaucrats got bent out of shape when Victor referred to the *country* of Taiwan. The Chinese consider Taiwan to be a renegade province, not an independent country. They feel that it is just a matter of time before Taiwan comes back into the fold. This remains a sore point to the government and citizens of the Peoples' Republic of China.

5-3. In his usual up-beat fashion, Manley's loud voice, animated facial expressions, and powerful hand gestures were overpowering the Thai women, who are extremely soft spoken and demure. They were interpreting his loudness and expressiveness as anger and being out of control. No wonder they didn't want to work for such a boss.

Chapter Six

6-1. Taiwanese, despite their great economic leap into the global economy, still retain a good deal of superstition. This is particularly true about certain numbers. Some primary numbers, associated with very negative things such as death or excrement, are to be avoided at all costs. Other numbers, associated with positive things such as money, growth, and wealth, should be used in house addresses, license plates, and telephone numbers. In Taiwan the telephone company receives many requests for numbers that include the lucky numbers, leaving those with unlucky numbers unused. Thus, Kathryn's classmate believed strongly that unless he had a telephone number with lucky numbers in it, his business would be doomed from the start.

6-2. Thailand is a hierarchical society where relative social status is very important in everyday social relations. John, as a visiting foreigner, automatically enjoys high social status, particularly in comparison to domestic workers such as a maid. When John naively shook her hand, she mistook his good-natured gesture as mockery of her relatively low social status.

6-3. This cross-cultural misunderstanding between Mike and the Japanese scientist occurred because the role of the listener in Japan is substantially different from that in the United States. It is customary in Japan for listeners to use replies (called aizuchi in Japan) such as "hai" ("yes"), that signals that one is both listening and understanding.

Americans also do this by saying "yes" or grunting "umhum," but the Japanese use these to a much greater extent. Because Mike was not giving off any aizuchi, the Japanese scientist kept seeking reassurance that his message was getting across.

Chapter Seven

7-1. Giving knives as gifts in Argentina has a negative meaning. The giving of anything sharp, such as a knife or a pair of scissors, symbolizes severing, not starting or maintaining, a friendship or relationship. Charles' client was, thus, offended by his choice of gift.

7-2. Rod's Chinese colleague was an advocate of Feng Shui, an ancient Chinese philosophy, which calls for finding the most harmonious and auspicious place to live and work. Feng Shui dictates how a building should be built in order to have a smooth flow of positive energy. For example, the front door should face the east, not the west, which is associated with death. There are many such requirements for the physical features of a building if it is to conform to the principles of Feng Shui.

7-3. Despite all of Michael's qualifications, he had one personal characteristic working against him---his age. Since Germans equate age with experience and competence, corporate leaders and decisions-makers in Germany tend to be older than their American counterparts. Thus, Michael's relative youth and perceived lack of experience led the Germans to lack confidence in him and his company.

References

Andersen, Peter, "Explaining Intercultural Differences in Nonverbal Communication." IN Larry Samovar and Richard Porter (eds.), INTERCULTURAL COMMUNICATION: A READER (6th Ed.). Belmont, CA: Wadsworth Publishing, 1991, pp. 286-96.

Arrindell, Willem, "Femininity and Subjective Well-Being" IN G. Hofstede, et al (eds.), MANSCULINITY AND FEMINITY: THE TABOO DIMENSION OF NATIONAL CULTURES. Thousand Oaks, CA: Sage, 1998, pp. 44-54.

Barry, Dave, "Does Concept of Time Depend on Gender?" CHARLOTTE OBSERVER, November 22, 1998, p. 3-E.

Bello Nino Lo, ENGLISH WELL SPEECHED HERE. Los Angeles, CA: Price, Stern and Sloan, 1987.

Bernard, H. Russell, RESEARCH METHODS IN CULTURAL ANTHROPOLOGY. Newbury Park, CA: Sage Publications, 1988.

Besner, Patricia, "Watch Your Language." PACE, 9 (2), (March/April, 1982).

Birdwhistle, Raymond L., KINESICS AND CONTEXT: ESSAYS ON BODY MOTION AND COMMUNICATION. Philadelphia: University of Pennsylvania Press, 1970.

Black, J. Stewart, Allan Morrison, and Hal Gregersen, GLOBAL EXPLORERS: THE NEXT GENERATION OF LEADERS. New York: Routledge, 1999.

Brake, Terrence, Danielle Walker and Thomas Walker, DOING BUSINESS INTERNATIONALLY: THE GUIDE TO CROSS CULTURAL SUCCESS. Burr Ridge, IL: Irwin Professional Publishing, 1995.

Buck, R., THE COMMUNICATION OF EMOTION. New York: Guilford Press, 1984.

Christopher, Robert C., THE JAPANESE MIND. New York: Simon and Schuster, 1983.

Collins, Robert J., JAPAN-THINK, AMERI-THINK: AN IRREVERENT GUIDE TO UNDERSTANDING THE CULTURAL DIFFERENCES BETWEEN US. New York: Penguin Books, 1992.

Condon, John, WITH RESPECT TO THE JAPANESE: A GUIDE FOR AMERICANS. Yarmouth, Maine, Intercultural Press, 1984.

Condon, John and Fathi Yousef, AN INTRODUCTION TO INTERCULTURAL COMMUNICATION. Indianapolis: Bobbs-Merrill Company, 1975.

Cooper, Robert K. and Ayman Sawaf, EXECUTIVE EQ: EMOTIONAL INTELLIGENCE IN LEADERSHIP AND ORGANIZATIONS. New York: Grosset/Putnam, 1996.

Ervin-Tripp, Susan, "An Analysis of the Interaction of Language, Topic, and Listener." AMERICAN ANTHROPOLOGIST (special publication), 66, 1964, pp. 86-102.

Ferraro, Gary, CULTURAL ANTHROPOLOGY: AN APPLIED PERSPECTIVE. Belmont, CA: Wadsworth Publishing Company, 2001.

Ferraro, Gary, THE CULTURAL DIMENSION OF INTERNATIONAL BUSINESS (3rd Ed.). Upper Saddle River, NJ: Prentice Hall, 1998.

Foster, Dean Allen, BARGAINING ACROSS BORDERS: HOW TO NEGOTIATE BUSINESS ANYWHERE IN THE WORLD. New York: McGraw-Hill, 1992.

Friedl, John, and John E. Pheiffer, ANTHROPOLOGY: THE STUDY OF PEOPLE. New York: Harper and Row, 1977.

Friedman, Thomas, THE LEXUS AND THE OLIVE TREE: UNDERSTANDING GLOBALIZATION. New York: Farrar, Straus, and Giroux, 1999.

Geewax, Marilyn, "Aging Will Change U.S. 'Youth' Culture." THE CHARLOTTE OBSERVER, February 10, 1999, p. 17A.

Gesteland, Richard R., CROSS-CULTURAL BUSINESS BEHAVIOR: MARKETING, NEGOTIATING AND MANAGING ACROSS CULTURES. Copenhagen: Handelshojskolens Forlag, 1999.

Haber, Carol, BEYOND SIXTY-FIVE: THE DILEMMA OF OLD AGE IN AMERICA'S PAST. New York: Cambridge University Press,1983.

Hall, Edward T., THE DANCE OF LIFE: THE OTHER DIMENSION OF TIME. Garden City, NY: Doubleday, 1983.

Hall, Edward T., THE HIDDEN DIMENSION. Garden City: Doubleday, 1966.

Hall, Edward T., THE SILENT LANGUAGE. Garden City, NY: Doubleday, 1959.

Hall, Edward T. and Mildred R. Hall, UNDERSTANDING CULTURAL DIFFERENCES: GERMANS, FRENCH, AND AMERICANS. Yarmouth, Maine: Intercultural Press, 1990.

Hess, Beth, Elizabeth Markson, and Peter J. Stein, SOCIOLOGY. New York: Macmillan, 1993.

Hickerson, Nancy P., LINGUISTIC ANTHROPOLOGY. New York: Holt, Rinehart, and Winston, 1980.

Hofstede, Geert, CULTURE'S CONSEQUENCES: INTERNATIONAL DIFFERENCES IN WORK RELATED VALUES. Beverly Hills, CA: Sage, 1980.

Holmes, Ellen Rhoads and Lowell D. Holmes, OTHER CULTURES, ELDER YEARS. (2nd ed.). Thousand Oaks, CA: Sage Publications, 1995.

Kanter, Rosabeth Moss, WORLD CLASS: THRIVING LOCALLY IN THE GLOBAL ECONOMY. New York: Simon and Schuster, 1995.

Kim, Min-Sun, "A Comparative Analysis of Nonverbal Expressions as Portrayed by Korean and American Print-Media Advertising." In Judith Martin, Thomas Nakayama, and Lisa Flores (Eds.), READINGS IN CULTURAL CONTEXT. Mountain View, CA: Mayfield Publishing Company, 1998, pp. 206-217.

Klineberg, Otto, CHARACTERISTICS OF THE AMERICAN NEGRO. New York: Harper and Row, 1969.

Kluckhohn, Florence and Fred Strodtbeck, VARIATIONS IN VALUE ORIENTATIONS. Westport, CN: Greenwood Press, 1961.

Kupfer, Andrew, "How to be a Global Manager." FORTUNE, March 14, 1988, pp. 52-58.

Levine, Robert and E. Wolfe, "Social Time: The Heartbeat of Culture." PSYCHOLOGY TODAY. March, 1985, pp. 29-35.

Mehrabian, Albert, SILENT MESSAGES. Belmont, CA: Wadsworth, 1971.

Mitsubishi Corporation, TATEMAE AND HONNE: DISTINGUISHING BETWEEN GOOD FORM AND REAL INTENTION IN JAPANESE BUSINESS CULTURE. New York: The Free Press, 1988.

Moran, Robert T., Phillip R. Harris, and William G. Stripp, DEVELOPING THE GLOBAL ORGANIZATION: STRATEGIES FOR HUMAN RESOURCE PROFESSIONALS. Houston, TX: Gulf Publishing Company, 1993.

Morris, Desmond and Peter Collett, Peter Marsh and Marie O'Shaughnessy, GESTURES: THEIR ORIGINS AND DISTRIBUTION. New York: Stein and Day, 1979.

Nanda, Serena, "Arranging a Marriage in India." in THE NAKED ANTHROPOLOGIST. Philip DeVita (ed.). Belmont. CA: Wadsworth, 1992, pp. 137-43.

Napolitano, Carole S. and Lida Henderson, THE LEADERSHIP ODYSSEY: A SELF DEVELOPMENT GUIDE TO NEW SKILLS FOR NEW TIMES. San Francisco: Jossey-Bass Publishers, 1998.

Offermann, Lynn and Peta Hellmann, "Culture's Consequences for Leadership ." JOURNAL OF CROSS-CULTURAL PSYCHOLOGY 28(3), May, 1997, pp. 342-51.

Rhinesmith, Stephen H., "Global Mindsets for Global Managers" TRAINING AND DEVELOPMENT JOURNAL, October, 1992, pp. 63-68.

Rhinesmith, Stephen H., A MANAGER'S GUIDE TO GLOBALIZATION. Chicago: Irwin Professional Publishing, 1996.

Rosen, Robert, GLOBAL LITERACIES: LESSONS ON BUSINESS LEADERSHIP AND NATIONAL CULTURES. New York: Simon and Schuster, 2000.

Salmans, Sandra, "Industry Learns to Speaks the Same Language." INTERNATIONAL MANAGEMENT, April, 1979, pp. 45-47.

Salopek, J., "Is Anyone Listening?" TRAINING AND DEVELOPMENT, September, 1999, 53(9), pp. 58-59.

Satoshi, Ishii and Donald Klopf, "A Comparison of Communication Activities of Japanese and American Adults", paper given at the Communication Association of the Pacific, Tokyo, 1975.

Schlesinger, Arthur M., "What Then is the American, This New Man?" in THE CHARACTER OF AMERICANS: A BOOK OF READINGS. Michael McGiffert (ed.). Homewood, IL: Dorsey press, 1970, pp. 102-117.

Schor, Juliet, THE OVERWORKED AMERICAN: THE UNEXPECTED DECLINE OF LIESURE. New York: Basic Books, 1993.

Seager, J., and A. Olson, WOMEN IN THE WORLD ATLAS. New York: Simon and Schuster, 1986.

Senge, Peter, THE FIFTH DISCIPLINE: THE ART AND PRACTICE OF THE LEARNING ORGANIZATION. New York: Doubleday, 1990.

Senge, Peter, el al, THE FIFTH DISCIPLINE FIELDBOOK: STRATEGIES AND TOOLS FOR BUILDING A LEARNING ORGANIZATION. New York: Doubleday, 1994.

Shane, Scott, "Cultural Influences on National Rates of Innovation." JOURNAL OF BUSINESS VENTURING 8(1), 1993, pp. 59-73.

Shane, Scott, "Uncertainty Avoidance and the Preference for Innovation Championing Roles." JOURNAL OF INTERNATIONAL BUSINESS STUDIES. 26(1), 1995, pp. 47-67.

Speas, Kathy and Beth Obenshain, IMAGES OF AGING IN AMERICA: FINAL REPORT. AARP: Washington, DC., 1995.

Stewart, Edward C. and Milton J. Bennett, AMERICAN CULTURAL PATTERNS: A CROSS-CULTURAL PERSPECTIVE. Yarmouth, Maine: Intercultural Press, 1991.

Tannen, Deborah, THE ARGUMENT CULTURE: MOVING FROM DEBATE TO DIALOGUE. New York: Random House, 1998.

Tannen, Deborah, YOU JUST DON'T UNDERSTAND: WOMEN AND MEN IN CONVERSATION. New York: Morrow, 1990.

Trompenaars, Alfons, and Charles Hampden-Turner, RIDING THE WAVES OF CULTURE: UNDERSTANDING CULTURAL DIVERSITY IN GLOBAL BUSINESS (2ND ED.). New York: McGraw Hill, 1998.

Trompenaars, Alfons and Charles Hampden-Turner, THE SEVEN CULTURES OF CAPITALISM. New York: Currency/Doubleday, 1993.

Varenne, Herve, "America and I," in Philip R. DeVita and James D. Armstrong (eds.), DISTANT MIRRORS: AMERICA AS A FOREIGN CULTURE. Belmont, CA: Wadsworth Publishing, 1993, PP. 29-38.

Wills, Stefan and Kevin Barham, "Being an International Manager." EUROPEAN MANAGEMENT JOURNAL, 21 (1), March, 1994, pp. 49-58.

Wilson, Meena, et al, MANAGING ACROSS CULTURES: A LEARNING FRAMEWORK. Greensboro, NC: Center for Creative Leadership, 1996.

Yates, Brock, "An American Love Affair." LIFE MAGAZINE, (Collector's Edition),Winter, 1996, pp. 11-15.

Index

About the Author

Gary Ferraro, Professor of Anthropology, has taught at the University of North Carolina at Charlotte since 1971. He received his BA in history from Hamilton College and his MA and PhD degrees from Syracuse University. He has been a Fulbright Scholar at the University of Swaziland in Southern Africa and has served as a visiting professor of anthropology in the University of Pittsburgh's Semester at Sea Program, a floating university that travels around the world. He has conducted research for extended periods of time in Kenya and Swaziland and has traveled widely throughout many other parts of the world. He has served as a consultant for such organizations as USAID, the Peace Corps, and the World Bank. In recent years he has taken a more applied focus in his work by conducting cross-cultural training seminars for international business people, government officials, educators, and medical practitioners. From 1996 to 2000 Dr. Ferraro served as the Director of the Intercultural Training Institute at UNC-Charlotte, a consortium of cross-cultural trainers and educators from academia and business, designed to help regional organizations cope with cultural differences at home and abroad. In February of 2000, he became the president of Intercultural Associates, Inc., a private firm specializing in cross-cultural consulting and training.